Catching Stories

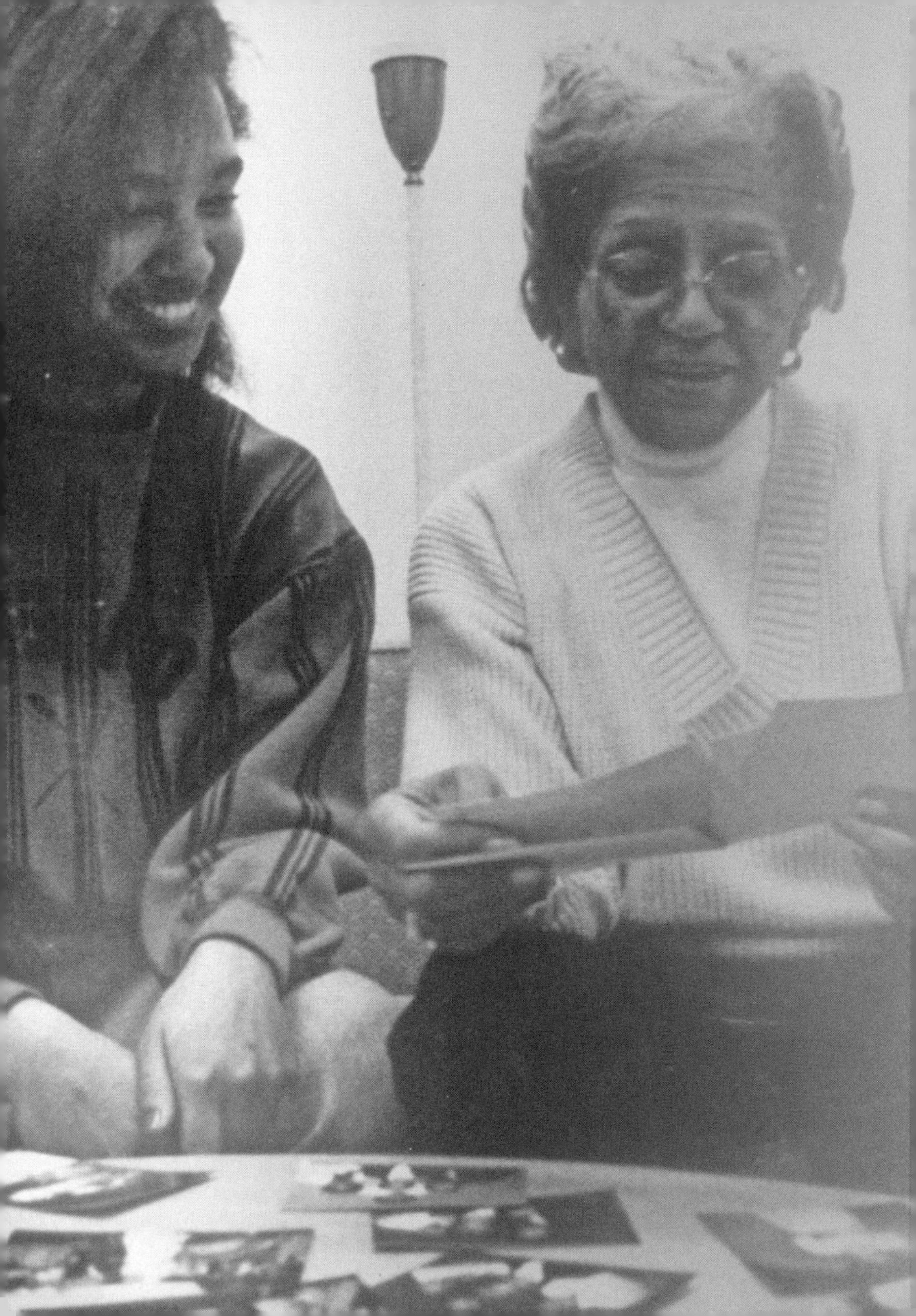

Catching STORIES

A PRACTICAL GUIDE TO ORAL HISTORY

Donna M. DeBlasio

Charles F. Ganzert

David H. Mould

Stephen H. Paschen

and Howard L. Sacks

SWALLOW PRESS ✦ ATHENS

Swallow Press / Ohio University Press, Athens, Ohio 45701
www.ohioswallow.com

Printed in the United States of America
Swallow Press / Ohio University Press books are printed on acid-free paper ∞ ™

16 15 14 13 12 11   5 4 3 2

Library of Congress Cataloging-in-Publication Data

Catching stories : a practical guide to oral history / Donna M. DeBlasio . . . [et al.].
p. cm.
Includes bibliographical references and index.
ISBN 978-0-8040-1116-7 (cloth : alk. paper)—ISBN 978-0-8040-1117-4 (pbk. : alk. paper)
1. Oral history—Handbooks, manuals, etc. 2. Oral history—Methodology. 3. Interviewing—Handbooks, manuals, etc. I. DeBlasio, Donna Marie.
D16.14C379 2009
907.2—DC22

2009005818

Contents

Preface

> "Oral history . . . can be a means for transforming both the content and purpose of history. It can be used to change the focus of history itself, and open up new areas of inquiry; it can break down barriers between teachers and students, between generations, between educational institutions and the world outside; and in the writing of history—whether in books, or museums, or radio and film—it can give back to the people who made and experienced history, through their own words, a central place."
>
> —*Paul Thompson, The Voice of the Past: Oral History*

Oral history levels the playing field of historical research. You don't have to be a professional historian or a political mover-and-shaker to do it. Anyone with the interest, time, resources, and some training can undertake interviews for an oral history project—in a community, school, senior center, church, mosque, or temple. Changes in technology have made quality digital audio recorders and video camcorders available and affordable. There are no age barriers; oral history projects have been done by sixth-graders and octogenarians. Most important, there are no educational barriers; you do not need a PhD to interview doctors, farmers, computer scientists, coal miners, or quilters, and to present your interviews in a book, documentary, or exhibition. The democratic nature of oral history also has a profound impact on the topics covered. Community-based historians are likely to select topics that resonate with their own lives and with the memories and experiences of people like themselves—their work, family, traditions, and beliefs.

This sense of connection is important because so often history can seem distant and unrelated to our lives, work, family, or community. That's hardly surprising because of the way history has been taught in many countries. Children are asked to remember and recite in chronological order lists of monarchs, presidents, wars, treaties, laws, and national events. The problem with history, in the oft-quoted phrase, is that it's "one damned thing after another."[1] Or, as David Lowenthal more elegantly put it in *The Past Is a Foreign Country,* "It is so customary to think of the historical past in terms of narratives, sequences, dates and chronologies that we are apt to suppose these things are attributes of the past itself. But they are not; we ourselves put them there."[2] Indeed, we did. Inhabitants of fourteenth-century France did not realize they were living in the Middle Ages. The four hundred thousand young people who gathered for a four-day music festival in August 1969 did not know they were part of the Woodstock Generation, a label that came to represent a set of social and cultural values, until journalists and historians told them they were.

Even if we still find the past easiest to describe in epochal lumps—from the Renaissance to today's global society—at least we've moved beyond the great man-significant event view of history, where most of the actors were male and white and performed on a national or international stage. The study of history in U.S. schools and universities now devotes more attention to social, economic, and cultural trends and to issues of gender, ethnicity, class, family, and community. Indeed, some critics claim that the pendulum has swung too far and that political, military, and diplomatic history are now so neglected that some college-educated Americans confuse the two world wars and do not know which side the United States backed in Vietnam.

Almost all this history is written by academics and journalists or by the historical actors themselves—the politicians, generals, social activists, and pop-culture icons. As history, it can be read, learned, debated, or adapted into a TV documentary or drama. But it's still the work of experts with PhDs, careers in public service, or some claim to popular fame or notoriety. It's not history that most people can practice.

Enabling more people to practice history has always been the mission of the authors of this guide. We are committed to help people—from professional historians to community volunteers—add oral history skills to their toolkit of methods and give them the confidence to take on new projects. That's the primary audience for *Catching Stories*—people who want to research the histories of their families, neighborhoods, businesses, religious, professional and social groups. The guide will also be useful to college professors and students who plan to use interviews in their research. There are excellent books that examine oral history from a theoretical perspective, and these works have helped us to think analytically about the discipline. But ours is a practical guide.

As a teaching team, we first came together in 2000 as Ohio prepared for its 2003 bicentennial celebration. With community history projects under way across the state, the Ohio Historical Society (OHS) and Ohio Humanities Council (OHC) offered a series of workshops on how to do local history projects. Donna DeBlasio, David Mould, Steve Paschen, and Howard Sacks conducted one-day oral history workshops entitled Tell Your Stories, Preserve Your Past. OHS and OHC then brought us together to lead a more intensive three-day summer oral history institute. The institute debuted at Youngstown State University in 2001 and has been held on the campus of Kenyon College, Ohio, every year since then. Over the years, we have worked with more than two hundred participants from across the United States and overseas.

We open *Catching Stories* with the same question we pose at the first session of the institute: Why do oral history (chapter 1)? We then provide a step-by-step process for planning a project (chapter 2) and discuss the ethical issues oral historians face as they enter the living rooms—and the lives—of their interviewees (chapter 3). In chapter 4, we outline legal issues, including defamation, copyright and release forms, the sealing of interviews, and human subjects research. In chapter 5, we examine the interview from several perspectives—as a transaction, as historical evidence, and as performance—before providing practical tips on arranging and conducting interviews. Chapter 6 describes the process and challenges of transcribing oral history. And whereas other oral history guides give short shrift to technical issues, we devote two full chapters (7 and 8) to the principles of audio and video, providing advice on equipment and offering practical tips on how to obtain clear sound recordings and well-composed pictures. Because technology is always changing, it's tempting to skip this topic and offer the weak argument that any information published will be out of date. Machines and models certainly do change, but the physics of sound and light and the principles of analog and digital recording do not. Our experience is that oral historians both want and need to understand the technology and the language of the media they use. In chapter 9, we cover the basics of archiving oral history. Chapter 10 provides guidance on where to look for funding, how to approach foundations and other granting agencies, and how to put together a competitive proposal. Finally, we outline options for presenting—from traditional exhibits to multimedia and online presentations (chapter 11).

Each member of the team comes to this project from a different background. Donna is a trained historian who worked in the applied history field with the OHS and Cincinnati Museum Center before joining the faculty at Youngstown State University in 1999. David's academic training is also in history, but he teaches communications at Ohio University and has worked as a newspaper reporter, TV news writer, public radio producer, and documentary producer; he has also worked overseas, mostly in Asia. Steve began his professional career as a landscape architect, returned to school to study history and library science, became a museum director, and is now an academic archivist at Kent State University with a fondness for local and regional history. Trained as a sociologist, Howard has spent much of his career exploring community life in rural central Ohio—its arts, agricultural practices, cultural diversity—and forging this work into a variety of public projects. To provide additional information and perspectives on technical issues, we invited Professor Charles Ganzert of Northern Michigan University, a former public radio producer, to join the team. Chuck teaches audio production and media law, manages a recording studio, advises a student radio station, and has produced award-winning live music and interview shows with his students.

With five authors, there are five voices. These voices emerge in the issues each of us considers important and in our different writing styles. We agree on many issues and practices in oral history and bring different yet complementary perspectives to others. We believe this diversity enriches the work.

We would like to thank the colleagues and friends who have supported the Oral History Institute, including our long-term sponsor, the OHC, its director Gale Peterson, its program officers Frank Dunkle and Jack Shortlidge, and J. D. Britton and Andy Verhoff of the OHS, who helped launch the institute. Special thanks go to John A. Neuenschwander, professor of history at Carthage College (Wisconsin) and author of *Oral History and the Law,* and to Edward Lee, associate professor in the Moritz School of Law at the Ohio State University, for their detailed review of the chapter on legal issues.

Most of all, we thank the many community historians with whom we have worked over the years. Our greatest reward is to see an oral history project begin to transform and inspire a community, bringing people together to learn about a shared past. This book is dedicated to the thousands of oral historians all over the world who are making history relevant again by catching stories.

Donna M. DeBlasio

Charles F. Ganzert

David H. Mould

Steve H. Paschen

Howard L. Sacks

NOTES

1. Although the phrase is usually attributed to the British historian Arnold J. Toynbee, he criticized such mechanical and deterministic approaches. See Toynbee, *A Study of History,* abridged by David C. Somervell (New York: Oxford University Press, 1947), 267.

2. David Lowenthal, *The Past Is a Foreign Country* (New York: Cambridge University Press, 1985), 219.

Chapter One

Why Do Oral History?

By Howard L. Sacks

A myriad of projects capture the interest and energies of individuals and organizations conducting oral history projects nationwide. Last week, the Women's Circle of Shiloh Baptist voted to document this inner city church's hundred-year history. Ed Panello's veterans group has expressed interest in preserving the experiences of soldiers who fought in World War II. The Springfield Historical Society's recent recruits have proposed collecting materials on the railroad industry that once shaped community life. And Zevan Corporation's business manager believes it's a great idea to document the trade skills of the company's machinists.

But why bother? To those devoted to doing oral history, the answer may seem self-evident; indeed, just posing the question may border on blasphemy. But the answers to this question are, in fact, many and complex; those contemplating an oral history project often jump into research without carefully considering their motivations and goals. Why do you want to do this work? What do you hope to accomplish? Taking time to understand why you're doing oral history is essential to the success of your project. Be sure to bring other interested parties into the

Failing to first ask *why* inevitably results in one of two all-too-common outcomes. You end up with a box of worthless materials that gather dust on a shelf because nobody knew what to do with the stuff. Or you find that the public isn't interested because you assumed that everyone would share your sense that the subject is worthwhile.

conversation, no matter how confident you are of the rightness of your motivations.

It's all too easy to jump ahead to what is undoubtedly the most exciting part of any oral history project—sitting down with people to conduct interviews. But failing to first ask *why* inevitably results in one of two all-too-common outcomes. You end up with a box of worthless materials that eventually gather dust on some shelf because nobody really ever knew what to do with the stuff once it was collected. Alternatively, you debut your project only to find that the public isn't interested because you assumed, in error, that everyone would share your sense that the subject is inherently worthwhile.

WHO'S INVOLVED?

Any oral history project involves a variety of participants, each with his or her own needs and interests. Why do you *as an individual* want to do oral history? Perhaps you're an archivist or librarian, in which case this work may constitute part of your occupation. If you're a student, oral history research might well contribute to a paper or thesis leading to an academic degree. Volunteers, who conduct many oral history projects, participate because they're interested in the subject, want to develop new skills, or relish a personal challenge.

I teach a seminar on fieldwork at Kenyon College, a small undergraduate institution in rural Ohio. Most of our students come from metropolitan areas; to them, the midwestern rural landscape seems a world apart from the skyscrapers and manicured suburbs of New York, Chicago, or Los Angeles. The students who find their way to my seminar are typically motivated by a desire to engage the surrounding community, to learn something about a rural world that they are unlikely to encounter at any other point in their lives.

As I fashion each project that becomes the focus of my students' fieldwork, I'm careful to keep their personal motivations in mind. Experience tells me that their enthusiasm for and commitment to the research will be greatest if the work addresses the interests that brought them to the course in the first place.

Ignoring individual interests—and agendas—can contribute to several difficulties in the research process. One crucial decision in any project is determining who will conduct the interviews that lie at the core of any oral history effort. Let's say that a town bicentennial committee plans to produce a film documenting local history. A person joins the project mainly to impress others with her great personal knowledge of the community or to shape the town's image as portrayed in the film. Recognizing that this person is likely to impose her views on others, the good project planner does not assign her to the role of interviewer; instead, that person is asked to help in other areas where she can be productive but not quite so directive.

Individuals do the work of oral history, but projects are typically organized and sponsored by *groups* or *organizations*. Like individuals, groups have their own reasons for doing things; if they're formally constituted as an organization, those reasons should be articulated in a mission statement. For example, Kenyon's Rural Life Center, which I direct, seeks "to promote educational, scholarly and public projects that enhance the quality of life in Knox County, Ohio." A local historical society takes as its charge the documentation and preservation of life in a particular community. A community college is devoted to the educational enrichment of its students. An ethnic organization may be created to provide its members with economic opportunities and to enhance the public image of the group.

It's important to match the goals of your project with those of the organizations you hope to work with. Bear in mind that most organizations don't have "conduct an oral history project" as a stated goal. Therefore, you will likely be in the position of having to enlist the support of a cooperating institution. Often, the impulse is to explain why *you* wish to do a project. But to

Most organizations don't have "conduct an oral history project" as a stated goal. To be truly effective, focus on how the project addresses the *group's* central concerns. How does this work benefit the organization, tie into its mission, and enhance its value?

be truly effective, focus instead on how the project addresses the *group's* central concerns. How does this work benefit the organization, tie into its mission, enhance its value?

Kenyon College has lent its support to public oral history projects in part because it reaps numerous and demonstrable benefits from them. In offering students the opportunity to seriously engage rural life, Kenyon distinguishes itself from other institutions competing for qualified students; its admissions office highlights this opportunity in its publications and campus tours. Ongoing contact with the surrounding rural community affords students a unique experience of diversity. And the public projects emanating from our oral history research improve town-gown relations.

Most important to planning any oral history project is the perspective of the *community under study*. We know why we want to do this project and how our work complements the interests of a sponsoring organization. But how does the proposed oral history project address the needs and interests of those who will participate as subjects and the broader groups they represent? At the very least, those you intend to interview must be sufficiently interested in the project to cooperate. But the best oral history projects do more than this by taking time to identify and respond to community concerns.

In developing a documentary project on the history of our county's African American community, my students and I spent several months becoming better acquainted with local black life. We attended area churches, visited locations significant to black history, and engaged in casual conversations with the area's African American inhabitants. We then invited several dozen black residents to Kenyon for a meeting to discuss the character of local black life. In the course of that meeting, we learned several things that helped define the project to follow.

These residents expressed a clear desire to have the wider community appreciate their history. As one gentleman put it, "Black folks have been here as long as white folks, and it's time they understood the contribution we've made." They lamented the fact that their history appeared nowhere in the county's historical society museum and wanted that to change. This aspect was very important to those of us contemplating the project. We knew that invisibility—maintaining a low community profile—is a tactic minority groups frequently use to avoid prejudice and discrimination, and we were concerned at the outset that local black residents might resist publicly telling their story.

Shortly before our gathering, two elderly members of the black community had passed away. Both of these individuals had possessed knowledge about the community that extended into the nineteenth century; beyond the keen sense of personal loss, residents also felt the loss of a connection to their collective past. Clearly, these sad events prompted a strongly felt need to document their history.

But their motivations to participate in an oral history project related to the present as much as the past. Many older residents noted a decline in activities that previously had brought the community together. Ironically, the end of segregation reduced the pressure for exclusive black gatherings—whether it was through the enforcement of "colored day" at the community pool or the creation of black-sponsored clubs and social events. The migration of youth to the city in the 1960s further eroded the black community. There was a hunger for something that would enhance sociability and community identification.

Hearing this community perspective gave us a clear direction for the project. We would gather oral histories and other materials and fashion them into an exhibit that would travel to area schools, libraries, and churches before its permanent installation in the county historical society museum. As part of our effort to collect materials, we would hold a public event at the county public library, inviting everyone with relevant recollections, photographs, or other materials to share what they had. Taken together, the research and resulting exhibit

Oral history projects must address the needs and interests of all the participating groups:

- individuals conducting the research
- sponsoring organizations
- communities under study
- audiences for the project

would begin to document a community's past and support its present.

This example calls to mind an additional participant, the *audience*. Needless to say, any public oral history project must pay attention to its audience. Oftentimes, the primary concern is to attract people to your project. Here, too, identifying the interests of those involved can enable you to fashion a project of interest to others.

One useful way to think about projects and their audiences involves the distinction between *inreach* and *outreach*. Inreach projects are directed primarily to participants in the phenomenon you are studying. A project documenting the history of a fraternal lodge or church, for example, would be of interest primarily to members of that organization. Because your audience has a direct connection to your subject, they're likely to be enthusiastic. Indeed, many of the people in your audience may have participated in the research itself (a fact you should be sure to acknowledge in any project debut).

Think about projects as *inreach* and *outreach*. Inreach projects are directed primarily to participants in the phenomenon you are studying. Outreach projects introduce something to audiences who may not have direct familiarity with the subject.

There was a strong inreach component to our local black history project, and some of the audience members' motivations were typical of this type of project. When the exhibit debuted at the county historical society, the entire black community was in attendance, a crowd larger than any the museum had ever encountered. People took great pleasure in seeing old photographs of family and friends, many now departed. They read interview excerpts on the exhibit panels with great interest; what our interviewees said provided direct insights into their lives. Taken as a whole, the exhibit offered tangible validation of the community and generated a strong sense of pride.

In contrast, outreach projects are designed to introduce something to audiences who may not have direct familiarity with the subject at hand. It's often harder to generate public interest in this type of project because people don't immediately see its relevance to their daily lives. As a result, the narrative approach and content presented will of necessity be somewhat different from those of an inreach project. You may need to explain more explicitly the significance of the project and be sure not to assume the audience is already familiar with the details of whatever you're exploring. Audiences for an outreach project come for their own reasons—to be entertained, to learn something new, or to express a general interest in history.

At this point, we can begin to appreciate the importance of asking why you should conduct a project. First, doing oral history is hard work that requires significant resources. How many projects have initially attracted a horde of interested volunteers, who subsequently disappeared in the course of training and interviewing? Unless the activities are designed to be personally fulfilling, volunteers are unlikely to endure the hard work and logistical details that accompany any oral history project.

Second, your goals for doing oral history affect every step of the research process. Consider these questions: Whom should I interview, and what questions should I ask? How many individuals? What other materials do I need to collect? What will I do with the materials once they're collected? How will I present my work to the public? Without a clear sense of mission and purpose, your responses to these and other questions will tend to be ad hoc, making it difficult to fashion a thorough and cohesive project.

Third, knowing why you are doing this is essential to communicating with the public. When you contact prospective interviewees, you'll need to convincingly explain why you're engaged in this effort if you want to solicit their cooperation. To generate community interest, I've always found it valuable to obtain local media coverage early on in the project; that way, people will know something about my project before I begin to line up participants. Here, too, it's important to clearly state your motivations for embarking upon the project.

Fourth, funding organizations require a clear explanation of your reasons for proposing the project. Grant applications typically include the why question as part of the written narrative that accompanies any funding request. But even if the process is more informal, you'll need to thoughtfully convey your goals to anyone you hope will support your work.

Fifth, having a clear idea of your project goals is essential to evaluating your success. Funding agencies invariably require that you identify assessment strategies. But whether or not you receive outside funding, careful reflection on the impact of your effort should constitute the final step of every oral history project.

Understand why you are conducting oral history so that you can

- maintain participant enthusiasm
- guide decision-making
- communicate effectively with the public
- make the case for funding
- evaluate the success of your project

WHAT'S IT ALL ABOUT?

Participants' motivations constitute an important backdrop for defining your oral history project. It's important as well to think about the ultimate purpose of the effort with the help of three different models: *documentary, interpretive,* and *civic.*

The Documentary Approach

Documentary projects seek to preserve and present information about a topic. They are principally descriptive. Think, for example, of any so-called documentary film. The fundamental question is: What is it?

Preservation is a fundamental goal of any good oral history project. Gather the stories that provide a window to the past and save them for posterity. That's why careful preservation of the valuable physical materials collected in any project—audio and video recordings, photographs, artifacts—is such an important issue, treated at length later in this volume.

In public history projects, a primary outcome of documentary efforts involves sharing what was learned with a broader community. Rarely, except perhaps in genealogical research or personal family histories, is documentation conducted for the sake of those conducting the project alone. Not long ago, I attended a presentation sponsored by my local historical society about Hiawatha Park in Mount Vernon, Ohio, Knox County's largest town and county seat. The presenter, an elderly gentleman who had developed an interest in the subject, showed slides from his collection of postcard photographs of the park, illustrating the various buildings and activities to be found there. We learned that Hiawatha Park was a popular amusement park from 1890 until World War I, that an electric trolley transported visitors from the train station in nearby Mount Vernon, and that the original site of the park is now the county fairground.

The presentation prompted comments from the audience of mostly older men and women. Some offered childhood reminiscences or stories they had heard from their parents. One gentleman noted that a small building from the original park, with its Victorian gingerbread decoration, still stands amid the current barns and exhibition buildings at the fairground.

All this is interesting enough. But why is it important to us now? There was more to know—to understand—about Hiawatha Park that didn't make it into the presentation. As a suburban retreat frequented by travelers from Akron, Canton, and Columbus, the park illustrates that the American urge to escape from the city had already begun to express itself more than a century ago. The inclusion of a new 1,500-seat theater on the grounds suggests how important entertainment and culture had become in a small midwestern town.

Focusing exclusively on descriptive detail, as this gentleman did, missed the park's broader significance. Local historical museums can make similar choices in their exhibits. Oftentimes, these museums are stuffed with interesting artifacts collected in the area. But no attempt is made to say anything about these items apart from their brief description (e.g., "1862 Knox County Quilt") and physical collection in areas designated for the kitchen, parlor, church, and entertainment.

One particular type of documentary research is worth noting because it underlies many oral history projects. Speaking of his own discipline, the scholar Bruce Jackson called it "salvage folklore." Such projects are defined by a strong motivation to document some phenomenon that is fast disappearing—a dying craft or occupational tradition, or the recollections of aging veterans.

Certainly, this work has value. Anyone who has lost an elderly contact to death is keenly aware of the fact that some interviews, like some projects, should not be delayed. The sense of losing knowledge can be a powerful motivator directing oral history research. But as Jackson rightly notes, when oral history involves a last-ditch effort to capture something before it disappears, it's often already too late to find the sources needed for effective documentation.

Salvage efforts may imply that anything old is worth preserving, but, of course, that just isn't so. Not all historical material is equally important. We all distinguish the trivial from the significant in our everyday lives. Surely, one important goal of oral history is to demonstrate that our everyday experiences and perspectives *are* important, that history is not just the purview of the rich and powerful. But there is a danger in setting out to document something simply because it might soon be lost without carefully considering the value of the enterprise.

One criterion of value to consider is the contemporary significance of the material you want to collect. History buffs (which is to say, everyone who has considered doing oral history) are inclined to find the past inherently interesting. But as any high school history teacher can attest, that is an attitude not universally shared. As a society, we are drawn far more easily to whatever is new and improved than to the lives of our grandparents.

I once organized a national tour of working cowboys who practiced traditions—storytelling, poetry, and music—long associated with that line of work. In the current context, we can think of their concerts as public oral history performances. We called the tour The Old Punchers Reunion and emphasized the connection to history with publicity materials featuring old pictures of working cowboys. The tour was a success, but in the process we learned that history per se doesn't always sell. The next time around, we renamed it The Cowboy Tour and gave the publicity a more contemporary look. The public was drawn to appreciating the richness of their own world, which includes cowboys who recite poetry and do rope tricks.

In that same vein, documentary projects are often most effective and attract the largest audiences when they relate to contemporary issues. As our county bicentennial approached, a local video company researched and produced a series of films on local history. The first film took a purely descriptive approach, identifying major historical events organized along a linear timeline. But subsequent films developed a historical narrative in relation to current community concerns. For example, the film on education provided a historical context for issues such as school funding, curriculum, and building consolidation. People took interest, not because few could recall the days of one-room schools, but because history informed their current lives as individuals and as a community.

The urge to preserve history before it's gone can also skew our interest solely toward the oldest members of a community or group. Retired workers, church elders, and long-term residents certainly provide rich information and valuable perspectives on the past. But history extends to the present moment, and its subjects include the young as well as the old. If we ignore today's youth, we lose that stage of life and its distinctive worldview from the historical record or receive it only indirectly through hindsight.

The Interpretive Approach

The second model for doing oral history, the interpretive approach, builds on the descriptive, interpreting the character and significance of what is being documented. Interpretation is the essence of any humanities project. In the broadest sense, interpretive projects explore meaning within the human condition. It's easy to see that we can benefit from understanding, with interpretation, what life was like for soldiers in Iraq or the Korean War. But we can also find value in the everyday experiences of family farmers or office workers or churchgoers. Simply put, interpretive projects fashion the material they collect to answer the question: Why does this matter?

We can capture the difference between these models by considering two hypothetical captions to a photograph included in an exhibit. The picture shows a woman standing at a table, operating a machine. A descriptive caption might read: "Catherine Brown, at her home operating a Verso grinder to prepare canned tomatoes, ca. 1999." There's good descriptive detail here, and the information clearly locates the photograph in space and time. A more interpretive caption might also include this sentence: "In the years before convenience foods, many women preserved fresh local foods to feed their families through the winter months." We might have reached this conclusion from interviews with Brown and her contemporaries. This sentence uses the photograph to raise broader issues worth considering—our changing food habits, the evolution of women's roles, and the impact of new technologies and economies in our lives.

Publicly, interpretive projects aim less to answer that question than to generate a dialogue about it. In the local black history exhibit, stories we had collected made it clear that we would have to include some commentary about racism in our community. Interestingly, black residents differed on the extent to which racism existed in the county. Those who lived here before the civil rights movement of the 1950s and 1960s spoke readily about their experience of racial discrimination, and they expressed different responses to it. Younger residents and those who settled in the area after 1970 had a different set of life experiences, of course. So interpretively, the questions to explore were: Is racism a part of our community? In what ways?

We chose to include comments reflecting diverse experiences, something that stimulated public discussion about this important issue among blacks and across the community.

The Civic Approach

The third model uses oral history to facilitate civic action. Of course, generating public dialogue is essential to this goal; it constitutes the consciousness-raising that lays the groundwork for any social movement. But what distinguishes civic oral history projects is not their revolutionary zeal but their close connection to a civic goal of the sort that emerges in town hall gatherings, city planning discussions, and group meetings. Oral history projects can promote culinary or historic tourism, assist on a historic building restoration effort, or contribute to the continuation of a local craft skill that has economic value and helps define the community.

> Oral history projects may be *documentary, interpretive,* or *civic* in character. Documentary projects preserve and present information about a topic. An interpretive project emphasizes the meaning and significance of what is being collected. Civic oral history projects advance an expressed community goal.

Civic projects can also address social problems. When urban sprawl brought increasing numbers of new residents to central Ohio, a new conversation emerged about the nature of the community. Long-standing residents didn't consider the recent arrivals real Knox Countians because they didn't know the history of the area as did those born and raised here. For their part, newcomers often found the local folks rather standoffish. The division that developed along this line began to manifest itself in public debates about such issues as taxes, educational reforms, and land preservation.

My fieldwork students and I had read a wonderful book, *Endangered Spaces, Enduring Places,* by anthropologist Janet Fitchen, about changing life in rural upstate New York. Having encountered the same tensions in her fieldwork, she suggested that a common symbol might serve as the vehicle to unite community factions. The Kokosing River, which begins in and winds throughout Knox County, had just been designated an Ohio State Scenic River; there was a lot of buzz about that. Schools, businesses, and clubs take the Kokosing as their name, and nearly everyone relates to the river in some way. School classes make trips there, artists paint there, towns and villages line its banks, farmers plant in its fertile bottomland, and most of us drink its water.

We decided to select thirteen sites along the river that captured different moments of the region's history—the site of an early gristmill, a six-generation farm, a campground and canoe livery, and Kenyon's new environmental center, for example. At each site, we collected stories from those connected to it—young and old, natives and newcomers. We released *Life along the Kokosing* as a booklet with pictures and narrative about each location and an accompanying compact disc containing excerpts from our interviews about each site. The booklet included a map so people could literally travel the route or take an imaginative tour from the comfort of their living room.

Local radio stations played the series, and we think it did prove to be a useful learning tool for some residents. But it achieved unexpected impact when civic groups and organizations quickly took it up for promotional uses. Mount Vernon's downtown visitors bureau distributed the booklet to promote tourism and to introduce the community to prospective businesses that might develop here. The Ohio Department of Natural Resources promoted it in their publications to enhance appreciation for river corridors. Kenyon's environmental center employed it to develop public understanding about the connections between the natural and social environment.

Why do oral history? The work you do can be used for many different purposes. Understanding your broad purpose will enable you to conduct a project that ultimately serves your goals.

FOOD FOR THOUGHT

As we have seen, oral history projects can have many purposes—to document, to interpret, to contribute to civic action. These can all be part of a single project, or they can arise at various stages of a project. To illustrate this, I want to explore a multifaceted initiative that has been going on for nearly fifteen years called Food for Thought. Today, Food for Thought involves a countywide effort to build a dependable local market for foods produced in the area. But its roots lie in an oral history project that continues to inform community action.

In 1993 I launched a three-year oral history project to document and interpret family farming and its connection to rural life in Knox County. As someone with a long-standing interest in the community surrounding Kenyon College, I recognized that agriculture figured centrally in all aspects of this area's life. Most academic work about agriculture at that time, which emanated from agriculture schools at land-grant universities, limited its view to unraveling farm economics and finding technological solutions to current agricultural problems. These were important issues, but we also wanted to understand how farmers felt about the land, the ways in which farming shaped social relationships, and the values that prevailed in an agricultural community. We wanted, in short, to put the culture back in agriculture, to investigate not only farming but also the very meaning of community.

My students began by reading about local farm life in the daily newspaper and in historical documents and by visiting feed mills, implement dealerships, and livestock auctions. In the process we met several farmers and visited their farms. Around Thanksgiving we invited several farm families to the campus for a Sunday dinner, followed by an informal conversation about farm life.

These family farmers articulated that they felt underappreciated and misunderstood. Even in a rural community, they observed, few residents were still directly involved with agriculture. As a result, even their own neighbors often understood little about the hard work involved in producing the nation's food supply or the serious challenges facing small-scale farming. The farmers were very proud of their family farming traditions,

Students from the Rural Life Center at Kenyon College interview an extension agent for a project on family farming in Knox County, Ohio. Such projects not only give students experience in research, interviewing, and presentation but also help them understand the economics and culture of rural communities. *Courtesy of the Rural Life Center, Kenyon College*

some of which extended back six generations on the same plot of land, and they wanted people to know their story. But the strong sense of independence that attracts many people to farming meant it was unlikely that the farmers would enter the public arena on their own initiative.

The Family Farm Project thus developed both to document family farming and to stimulate public dialogue about farming and its relationship to community life. At the center of our work was the collection of dozens of interviews with farm families and others tied to agriculture. From this rich material we fashioned a variety of public projects, including a radio series, a Web site, a school curriculum, and countless public discussions and presentations.

Sometimes, intervening current events can transform oral history. As the Family Farm Project gained momentum, local civic leaders began to voice growing concern over the urban sprawl that was increasingly evident on the landscape. Suburban-style subdivisions were replacing cornfields, bringing increased traffic, the loss of green space, and the loss of intimacy in social relationships. Community focus groups emerged to engage issues of preservation and how to constructively guide growth. Fortuitously, residents started a broad discussion of the community just as the Family Farm Project was creating a public dialogue about the significance of agriculture in local rural life.

Out of these discussions emerged a county long-range plan that established community priorities and identified concrete initiatives to achieve desired ends. Knox Countians asserted as their top priority their wish to preserve the region's rural character. Drawing heavily on the work of the Family Farm Project, the resulting plan identified the preservation of family farming as central to achieving this goal. A college-based oral history project now informed a civic project to preserve and enhance the community.

The question now was *how* to preserve family farming. We knew from our many interviews that farmers felt a strong connection to the land—to making things grow and to the deep family roots. Their children wanted to stay close to agriculture; those who couldn't take over the family farm went to college to become large-animal veterinarians or learn computer technology they could use to assist farm operations. In most cases, farmers sold out to developers because they could no longer make an economic go of it in an increasingly centralized global market.

Working from our research, the Rural Life Center proposed several initiatives to build a local market for foods produced by area farmers, to be incorporated into the county's long-range plan: (1) publish a guide to local food products, enabling consumers to buy directly from farmers; (2) start a farmers' market in Mount Vernon's Public Square, creating an occasion for rural sociability and increasing economic activity in the business district, which was under stress from the rise of chain restaurants and big-box stores; and (3) encourage restaurants and other institutional food buyers to buy locally.

Members of the Hathaway family of Fredericktown, Ohio, pose with their John Deere tractor. The photograph, used in a project on family farming, reinforced stories from interviewees about the role of family and community relationships in small-scale farming in central Ohio. *Courtesy of Gregory P. Spaid*

All these efforts involved complex social engineering that goes beyond the subject of this volume. What is relevant here is the continuing role of oral history projects in all this work. The guide to local food products, called *HomeGrown,* included an essay on the history of local agriculture drawn from our interviews and related research. To promote the newly created farmers' market, we launched an oral history project to explore the significance of food in area residents' lives. *Foodways* included a series of essays, biographical sketches, and recipes, published in the newspaper in conjunction with the farmers' market, on topics including hunting and trapping, ritual foods, dining out, and feeding the hungry. We next mounted a traveling exhibit titled Where Does Our Food Come From? that explored the local food system from farm to table, based on fieldwork with farmers, processors, truck drivers, and chefs. The exhibit traveled to community fairs throughout Knox County and to statewide agricultural conventions.

These and other projects contributed to the goal of building a sustainable local food system by providing food for thought (hence the name of the project). For a generation, most consumers have taken the sources of their food for granted, making their food selections primarily on the basis of cost and convenience. If we are to build a local food system, consumers must think differently about the food they eat. They will have to appreciate how their food choices affect them as individuals and as a community. To these ends, oral history enables people to learn about food, farming, and their community in ways that translate directly to the decisions they make in their everyday lives.

THINKING AHEAD

Having a good sense of what motivates everyone involved and the goals you hope to achieve can orient the project as you confront particular issues and challenges. At the same time, you'll likely find yourself revisiting these questions at various points in light of new experiences, thus reshaping your original vision of the project. Complex, collaborative projects are dynamic in nature; starting out prepared, by considering these questions, will enable you to be thoughtful and flexible, assuring a successful, rewarding result for all involved.

Chapter Two

Planning an Oral History Project

By Stephen H. Paschen

A few years ago I got a call from the president of a local historical society. He asked me to meet with him to discuss the future of his organization's oral history project. We met at his institution's offices, where I was invited to look over the project materials. The project, which had begun three years earlier, was an open-ended effort to interview elderly longtime residents about their memories of the community. There was a box containing approximately forty-five audiocassette tapes, some of which were unlabeled and lying loose. The organization's president explained that after a few selected old-timers had been interviewed by historical society volunteers, the project had attracted hundreds of people interested in being interviewed. A list of interviewees was compiled, and volunteers were invited to borrow the tape recorder and a blank tape from the society's office and instructed to contact and interview interviewees from the list. After a few years, the volunteers had lost interest, and the project had dragged to a halt. Most of the prospective interviewees on the list had never been contacted or interviewed. There were no files relating to the project, no signed releases, and no transcribed interviews. The historical society board was planning to officially terminate conducting interviews and to craft the collected interviews into a community history book.

Too many oral history projects begin with good intentions only to lose momentum and become collections of undocumented cassette tapes relegated to storage in shoe boxes somewhere in the office closets of local historical societies or museums. Something goes wrong between project start-up and final disposition of the recordings and accompanying materials. This happens for a variety of reasons but often can be attributed to poorly focused topics and lack of proper planning and systematic implementation.

Oral history projects take many forms, such as research projects by doctoral students, community projects by historical societies, or interviews of presidential administration staffers. Projects may be driven by the impetus to gather raw data for documentaries, books, exhibits, and other products. But regardless of the scope or intended product, careful planning increases the likelihood of success. Most projects begin with an idea or topic, but a poorly conceived topic can prove fatal to the success of the project right from the beginning.

FOCUSING THE TOPIC

A few fundamental questions any oral historian must ask before investing time and effort in an oral history project should include: What information about a topic or person will oral history interviews provide? Why do you want to do oral history? Why is it important to do oral history? Oral history provides sources beyond the traditional kinds of information found in books, articles, and primary sources. It illuminates environments, perceptions, and feelings of individuals able to paint verbal pictures of all sorts of experiences such as workplace conditions, aspects of institutional living or foster care, and leisure activities. By focusing each topic through research

How Do Oral History Projects Fail?

- Failure to focus the topic
- Not enough resources
- Lack of community input
- Inadequate budget
- Too many interviewees

and discussion with interested professionals and volunteers, I have found that I can do a more effective job setting up a successful project.

Distinctive experiences of particular individuals or groups can be sampled through selection of interviewees sharing ethnic, cultural, religious, gender, family and extended family, and neighborhood experiences. Oral history holds the promise of providing color to fill the outlines of shared life experiences. But taking the time to study the intended topic will help to guide the project at the very beginning.

While still in the early stages of planning a project, it is wise to engage humanities scholars in the topic discussion. Finding scholars who are interested in your topic can be difficult, especially if there is no nearby college or university. Your state's humanities council or the National Endowment for the Humanities (NEH) can provide the contact information for humanities scholars in your region. Funding institutions such as the Ohio Humanities Council (OHC) or the NEH also usually employ program officers who are willing to discuss project ideas and give advice to make a project more desirable to grant review committees.

Regardless of the scope of a project, an effective early step is to form an advisory committee to discuss the topic, assist with project planning, and monitor progress throughout the life of the project. Committee members may be chosen for their expertise in the particular topic, technical knowledge, and planning skills, or they may be representative of the community or group from which interviewees will be selected. A committee of six to eight people can help shape project goals, assess and marshal the resources needed (including historical background materials), and review other viable programs to learn best practices. Again, having one or two humanities scholars serve on the committee will not only add to its credibility and balance, but also provide intellectual grounding for the project.

If there are committee members representing the community from which interviewees will be chosen, they can help identify the best pool of interviewees fitting the profile. The committee will serve as a reality check on the project, helping to define a doable scope, prepare a realistic budget, review the project plan, and monitor project progress so that it stays on track through completion.

Failure to focus the topic properly and limit the list of prospective interviewees to a manageable number frequently causes projects to bog down and fall behind schedule. Because so many potential interviewees might fit a broad topic, a project can become too open ended, losing energy and fading away over time. The best way to prevent this is to carefully draft an interviewee profile defined by age, gender, socioeconomic background, temporal (time period) factors, geography, or other characteristics. Interviewees may all be factory workers from a particular type of industry, professional people, labor union members or officials, students, women in the workplace, housewives, or may be defined by many other potential descriptors. Match an interviewee profile closely with the general topic or focus of the project.

PREPARING A WRITTEN PLAN

Preparation of a written, systematic plan increases the potential not only for a successful project but also for the creation of an oral history collection with enduring research value. Chapter 9 discusses why and how oral history can have enduring value for future researchers even if only a modest number of interviews are completed. The process of preparing a written plan is an important way to employ a consistent, rational methodology while setting standards and benchmarks for an effective program.

It is tempting sometimes, especially in the case of an oral history of limited scope, not to write a plan unless you are preparing a funding request. However, the process of writing a plan clarifies the work to be done, and it is advisable to submit a written proposal to your institutional governing board, supervisor, committee, or parent institution. A written plan will provide the raw material for a thorough, compelling funding proposal to a foundation, corporation, or other funding source. The act of wordsmithing even helps to provide effective phrases useful when marketing the project.

National Endowment for the Humanities (NEH)
http://www.neh.gov

Ohio Humanities Council (OHC)
http://www.ohiohumanities.org

Some funding institutions, such as the OHC and the NEH, provide well-conceived, time-tested project planning guidelines on their Web sites. You can find these and other planning guidelines through a simple online search.

A written plan may incorporate a number of sections to convey the concept, scope, timing, cost, and other factors for consideration. But for the purposes of this chapter, I will discuss the following general sections to be found in most proposals: project goals versus organizational mission, project description, resources needed, project schedule, record-keeping, final products, publicity, and budget.

Elements of a Written Plan

- Project goals versus organizational mission
- Project description
- Resources needed
- Project schedule
- Record-keeping
- Final product
- Publicity
- Budget

PROJECT GOALS VERSUS ORGANIZATIONAL MISSION

Although some oral history projects are stand-alone individual investigations, many more comprise single components of an array of programs an institution undertakes. When a university, museum, historical organization, or other parent institution contemplates a project, it is usually necessary to relate the project's connection to a larger institutional mission. It is easy to underestimate the expenditure of resources—personnel, supplies, equipment, and services—when undertaking even a modest oral history project. Therefore, the project's purpose must be in line with the institutional mission. For example, if a staff member of a historical society whose mission is to collect and interpret local (city) history is considering an oral history project to interview women war workers during World

War II, then the information to be gained from the interviews should be related significantly to that particular city's history.

A concise statement should be crafted to link the project's mission to the institutional mission. A more effective linkage is illustrated by the following example: "Akron Women at Work: The Homefront during World War II will create an oral history collection of interviews with women who worked in Akron's war industries, filling a gap in the documented history of this community, which is a primary mission of the Summit County Historical Society."

PROJECT DESCRIPTION

Once an oral history project has been effectively tied to the institutional mission, a carefully crafted, concise description of the project is the next step. An effective description will include some of the gaps in the historical record that will be filled by interviewees' personal testimony. Also compelling is a description of a social purpose, such as giving voice to a community or providing an ethnic group with a connection to its past. Paul Thompson, in *The Voice of the Past,* pointed out that through oral history a community participates in writing its own history: "Oral history . . . can give back to the people who made and experienced history, through their own words, a central place."[1]

A typical project of this type might be designed to capture the human story of the effects on residents of a blighted neighborhood when urban renewal and redevelopment altered the physical and social fabric of the area. Interviews with those who were displaced in the initial phases of slum clearance could provide a sense of how individuals and businesses reacted to these projects, perhaps contributing to a loss of the sense of place the neighborhood once enjoyed.

An advisory committee's discussion of issues like these, along with context that humanities scholars provide, will help to define the interviewee profile, an important component of the project description. The profile should be concise, defining geographical, temporal, and other criteria that limit the number of potential interviewees to a manageable project. In the example from the previous paragraph, an interviewee profile might be: "Individuals who lived or operated businesses within the Howard Street neighborhood between 1965 and 1968 and were compelled to relocate due to the city's inclusion of their neighborhood in the urban renewal project initiated during those years."

RESOURCES NEEDED

Often overlooked in the enthusiasm of developing an oral history project are the resources necessary for implementing the project. A written plan should include careful and thorough description of the types and amounts of equipment, supplies, personnel, and services that will be needed to complete the project. Later, the budget section of the plan should list each resource along with its corresponding estimated cost.

This crucial part of the plan must be done with practicality in mind. When planning a project, it is particularly difficult to determine how much time is needed to complete tasks, so accurate estimates of personnel costs pose a challenge. There are two ways to estimate personnel time more accurately.

First, and perhaps the most obvious, contact representatives of successful oral history projects already in progress. Well-run programs will give you reliable estimates of the time spent doing research, preparing for and conducting each interview, transcribing, indexing, and other aspects of personnel time.

Second, do practice run-throughs of different phases of the project. Effective interviews are the product of practice, so keep track of the time spent running through preliminary or practice sessions of researching, interviewing, transcribing, and other phases of the process. It is a good idea to repeat the exercise a few times because normally the first run-through does not provide a reliable example. Estimates of time often are conservative, and it is best to expect each phase to take two to three times as long as you anticipated.

You can determine equipment, services, and supplies based on availability and cost. These include such mundane but essential items as tapes, CDs or DVDs, recording machines, transcribing machines, paper and files, computers, copiers, and other supply costs, as well as transcribing and other fee-based services. Also include *in-kind* services, which are donated services provided free of charge by vendors or other businesses. Donated services such as transcribing provided by a friendly transcribing vendor or photocopying provided by a copier company—any services that individuals or companies might contribute free of charge to the project—can be estimated by the donor and should be included in the budget. Basic categories used in preparing a budget are discussed later in this chapter.

PROJECT SCHEDULE

Drafting a project schedule can be a daunting task, too. The first phases of a project, planning and preparation of materials prior to the first actual interviews, are relatively predictable and not hard to fit into a schedule. However, the latter phases constitute unpredictable time periods such as how long it will take to conduct the interviews themselves (you must allow time for travel, setup and breakdown of equipment, and follow-up correspondence), transcribing, making the collection of interviews usable for research and production of a final publication or audiovisual product.

Estimate the length of time for planning by selecting a date by which the governing board grants approval or by the deadline date for grant submission. Project planning then becomes a process working backward from these deadlines. If there is not sufficient time to meet such deadlines, it might be better to work toward the next deadline in the funding cycle or a later board meeting.

The difficulty estimating time spent actually conducting the interviews is complicated by human factors like an interviewee (or interviewer) illness, difficulties fitting into people's busy schedules, the weather, and other unavoidable delays. My colleague Howard Sacks instructs his oral history students to triple expected time estimates. Almost no project proceeds along a perfect schedule, so it is especially advisable not to be too ambitious in scheduling interviews. Every interview takes preparation before and processing after, so you should avoid making the project too large in its scope and expect some delays. Obviously it is very difficult to predict, but it is possible to take into account the time available and set some scheduling parameters for interviewers. Construct a basic project schedule, beginning with the major phases of the project (see sidebar).

Phases in a Typical Project Schedule

Phase 1: Research

Phase 2: Planning and budgeting

Phase 3: Recruitment of interviewees

Phase 4: Recruitment and training of interviewers

Phase 5: Interviews

Phase 6: Transcribing and records

Phase 7: Archiving

Plot out each phase of the project on a calendar by date, or include a period of weeks or months as benchmarks for the project staff and advisory committee to compare progress against.

One of the most effective ways to keep a schedule on track is to set calendared benchmarks for the program and project monitoring (a regular report on progress) by the advisory committee. For example, as part of phase 4, the project coordinator might report to the advisory committee that four interviewers have been recruited and trained.

Determining a fixed ending date for the project must be the goal of everyone involved in the project. It is usually disastrous for a project to be open ended. Open-ended projects tend to lose steam and grind to a halt after a time, never reaching a conclusion that produces a good usable research collection or product.

RECORD-KEEPING

Without effective record-keeping the value of an oral history project is destroyed. If there are no releases, the interviews cannot be used or accessed. If the recordings are not labeled or the interviewers are not identified on the recording, the interviews will likely be useless. All recordings and transcriptions, including those on physical media (such as audiotapes and videotapes) and digital media, should be marked clearly and consistently.

The project coordinator should monitor assignments made to interviewers so that interviewees are not kept waiting for excessive periods of time, a pattern that might cause the project to lose its credibility.

The details of basic record-keeping are discussed in chapter 9. But during the planning stage, the methods and forms required should be defined (typically an interview checklist, release, correspondence, and other materials specific to a particular interviewee, all filed alphabetically), the personnel who will be keeping the records identified, a location designated for the records to be stored during the project, and details included as to the final disposition (ownership and physical storage location) of the collection and/or product.

Marking the Recording

- Case (audiocassette or videocassette case or jewel case):
  1. Interviewee's last name, first name
  2. Date and place of interview
  3. Interviewer's full name
- Recording (audiotape or videotape, or CD):
  1. Interviewee's last name, first name
  2. Date and place of interview
  3. Interviewer's full name

FINAL PRODUCTS

The planning document should describe the anticipated final product(s) of the oral history project, whether the product consists of a collection accessible to researchers, an exhibit, a radio or television production, a live dramatic production, a publication, or some other interpretive work. Final products of oral history projects are discussed in chapter 8.

PUBLICITY

For several reasons, publicity is a necessary tool in oral history. A publicity plan conceived at the outset of a project can ensure that the project receives notice at its beginning, during its implementation, and at its conclusion. Just as the addition of humanities scholars to an advisory committee strengthens topic development, a publicity expert on the committee can ensure the marketing success of a project.

Community support, particularly within the segment(s) of the community from which representative interviewees will be selected, should be a publicity objective. Representative members of the advisory committee can be invaluable in planning and launching the project. Once a project has been planned, effective publicity can attract sponsorship—that is, funds—to underwrite its implementation. Publicity may be used to recruit potential interviewees, although depending upon its effectiveness it might actually attract more interviewees than a project can accommodate. It is obviously bad publicity for qualified people who fit the interviewee profile to be turned away disappointed. Publicity is an essential element in product debut, whether the product is a research collection, audiovisual production, publication, or live dramatic production.

Clearly, the timing, audience, and quality of publicity are central to its effectiveness. Having an expert as a member of the advisory committee can help lead to the desired results. The publicity plan should be carefully and clearly described in the written plan.

BUDGET

No project should be undertaken without an accurate appraisal of its cost. Most boards of trustees and funding institutions require a relatively detailed budget and do not want to guess at how you arrived at the numbers submitted.

Estimating equipment, services, and supplies can be done effectively as long as you take the time to research these costs carefully. Take into account the resources already available, prepare a detailed list of everything that will be needed down

Budget

Cost	*Description*
Supplies:	
$ ________	equipment cost (recorders, cameras, microphones, transcribing machines, etc.)
$ ________	recording media (audiotapes, videotapes)
$ ________	hard drives or server space
$ ________	tape storage (acid-free boxes)
$ ________	file boxes (archival acid-free record storage boxes)
$ ________	file folders (acid-free)
$ ________	Subtotal (supplies)
Consultant and Vendor Fees:	
$ ________	research (# hours at $/hr.)
$ ________	planning (# hours at $/hr.)
$ ________	interviews (# hours at $/hr.)
$ ________	transcribing (# hours at $/hr.)
$ ________	project administration (# hours at $/hr.)
$ ________	Subtotal (consultant and vendor fees)
$ ________	Total oral history project cost

to the number of file folders and audiocassettes. The old adage "the devil is in the details" holds true for cost estimating. Most boards and granting institutions check these details to see how thoroughly and accurately a project has been planned.

If outside vendors will be used for certain facets of the project, such as transcribing, tape dubbing, or indexing, the potential vendors can help accurately estimate these costs.

Personnel costs are often overlooked in budgets. If an organization devotes its own paid staff time to the project, there is obviously a real cost that is not being applied to other tasks. Boards of trustees in particular should pay close attention to how a staff is used. If even 20 percent of a curator's time is spent on an oral history project, that means 20 percent less time is being spent on accessioning backlogs, exhibits, acquisitions, or educational programs. The trade-off may not be worth the cost of using professional staff to implement the oral history project. Personnel costs, volunteer in-kind donations of time, and any outside help hired for the project should be present in the budget.

WRITING GRANT PROPOSALS

Writing grant proposals (funding) is covered in chapter 10, "Funding," but a few comments have their place here. Once a carefully written plan has been prepared, a compelling grant proposal will be much easier to produce. The work of preparing all the basic components of most grant applications is already done in the planning process and only needs to be customized into a specific grant proposal.

Finding grant funds should not be taken lightly or addressed at the last minute. Choosing the right funding institution depends on several factors that should be carefully researched, including specific funding deadlines and requirements, determining whether your organization meets eligibility requirements, identifying the kinds of activities and projects that funding institutions will consider, and procedures for applying. Often funding institutions allow prior contact with their staff to assess whether that institution would consider a project and what improvements could be made to the application to make it more fundable.

Many funding institutions require that you describe a method by which a funded project will be evaluated. This too can be a function of the advisory committee, particularly with the help of a committee member who has experience preparing evaluative techniques and instruments.

Above all, it is imperative to meet all deadlines and not to proceed hastily with grant applications. A late or sloppy application can doom the success of a grant submission right at the outset.

RESEARCHING THE TOPIC

No oral history interview can be effectively done unless each interviewer understands the overall context in which the topic fits. If an interviewee describes a local incident, geographical place, or contemporary national issue, the interviewer must think on the fly and be prepared to pursue intriguing subtopics that will illuminate the documented histories. Each project demands a measure of research and preparation on the part of the interviewer before he or she sits down opposite a person who experienced the events.

Unlike research for a historical article or book, research for an oral history project often has to be done on a shorter timeline. There are two basic steps to preparing historical materials for an oral history project: (1) finding and extracting pertinent information from historical sources and (2) preparing useful historical reference materials for interviewers.

FINDING SOURCES OF HISTORICAL INFORMATION

Historical research is done basically with two types of source materials. First and best known to most people are the secondary sources. These are the published books, articles, and brochures most people think of as historical sources. These contextual and specific works include national, local, corporate, institutional, and social history books, as well as smaller publications like brochures, pamphlets, and booklets. Some

Photographs help document interview themes, such as racial integration in the workplace. In the 1930s, more than a quarter century before the civil rights movement, New Deal programs brought African American and white workers together. In this integrated Works Progress Administration sewing room in Akron, workers take part in a social event. *Courtesy of the Summit County Historical Society*

secondary sources are particularly suited for local background history, such as corporate, institutional, and social histories about specific individuals and institutions.

The other type of source material is the real stuff of history—primary sources. These are the sources from which historians and other researchers craft their published works. Primary sources consist of first-hand archived information like records, personal papers and correspondence, business ledgers, photographs, diaries, and oral histories. These collections contain eyewitness testimony and stories described by people who experienced particular historical events and eras. Newspapers are defined as primary sources if the materials are contemporary accounts of the events reported, but sometimes they are not (as in the case of articles that do not represent contemporary reporting or opinions). Digital media must pass the test of firsthand reporting or commentary to be considered primary sources.

Both types of historical source materials can be found in a number of different types of repositories, including public libraries, historical societies, local and county museums, academic libraries and archives, and online repositories.

Public libraries sometimes have local history rooms with mixtures of artifacts (exhibits), books, and archival materials. Knowledgeable volunteers or paid staff members are usually on hand to assist with research. Display cases containing artifacts are sometimes arrayed throughout the library and are most effective when interpretive labels provide specifics and context. More sophisticated library exhibits are even sometimes augmented by exhibit catalogs containing useful historical information. Many libraries host regular meetings of local history groups such as genealogists, preservationists, and other specialists who might even become members of your oral history advisory committee. Occasionally libraries also house archival departments, which may have among their holdings maps, photographs, personal papers, and other types of local manuscript collections available to researchers. Generally primary source materials such as these do not circulate and cannot be taken from the library. Some may not even be duplicated if the donors of the materials placed restrictions on their use.

Historical societies, usually housed in local landmarks such as historic houses or other structures, sometimes have a limited or full library function. Often this type of institution focuses more narrowly on a city or county. These types of repositories may have hard-to-find local histories, compilations of primary sources, and newsletters containing historical information. Keep in mind that these organizations may have more limited hours of operation and may not have the latest source materials. Also, historical societies can be celebratory, nonanalytical, and noninterpretive organizations. The people assisting you may not even understand the notion of interpretation. Sources may seem to favor the famous, notorious, founding, or predominant classes within a locale. Many secondary sources published before the 1970s left whole groups of people unrepresented in local history. The publication of older city and county histories was often funded by paid subscription, so biographies may even exclude prominent people if they did not desire to pay the subscription fee to be part of the book. Corporate histories may be biased and celebratory in nature, too. Except for publications about pioneer days or the town's founding, everyday social history may not be represented either.

Local and county historical museums sometimes include small libraries and archives for public use, and are another possible resource for advisory committee members. These types of institutions may be the repositories of some materials that cannot be found anywhere else.

University libraries and archives often have extensive holdings of local or regional history books and other valuable sources. Academic archives may have collections of the papers of local notable citizens or local historical society collections under repository agreements. These repositories frequently have sources like census records, government (national and local) records, atlases, photographs, and many other useful sources and manuscript collections. Academic repositories typically provide online resources such as collections level lists, finding aids, and digital facsimiles of original documents and records.

The Internet, depending upon the topic of the project, can provide a wealth of resources. Internet sources should be held to the same standards of authenticity and accuracy as more traditional sources. Because anyone can put up a Web page and present information, it is advisable to measure each online source against the same questions that any other source must answer.

Wherever sources may be found, their credibility should always be verified if possible by proper citation and corroboration with other sources. Beyond issues of accuracy (sometimes local histories perpetuate legends and erroneous stories, although such stories reveal their own meanings) are the prob-

Assessing the Credibility of Sources

1. Who compiled the source? The quality of the information depends largely on the credentials of the author or Web site creator.
2. Are the primary and secondary sources from which the information is derived properly cited and findable? The information presented should be documented, well researched, and supported in related sources you can access yourself.
3. Is information presented as fact or opinion? Opinion presented as fact is less credible, especially if it is not designated as such.
4. Are grammar, punctuation, and spelling correct? Poorly written information is a sign of poorly researched and weakly interpreted materials.

lems and omissions of gaps in the historical record and unrepresented ethnic, minority, or gender groups.

Once sources have been located, typically there is a mass of material that must be condensed or summarized in a way that will be useful to interviewers preparing for their interviews. Keeping well-organized research notes with properly cited sources makes the information easier to use. The appendix to this book provides a simple method for keeping research notes.

PREPARING HISTORICAL BACKGROUND INFORMATION

Interviewers preparing specific questions for each interview must have some understanding of the historical topics behind the questions. It is not useful to prepare volumes of material and expect extensive study by the interviewers. What they really need are some materials condensed into a format that can be used for quick reference. A brief and concise narrative overview of the topic can give each interviewer an understanding of the basics of the topic. Also, historical outlines can pull together international, national, and local information from the same time period, providing context for the interviewee's testimony. Interviewers can have a richer understanding of the

Workers stamp out porcelain light fixtures on the assembly line at the Akron Porcelain and Plastic Company in the 1930s. Pictures of factory equipment and work can help interviewers draft informed questions and interpret answers that describe industrial processes. *Courtesy of the Akron Porcelain and Plastics Company*

temporal parameters of the project research if you provide detailed topical outlines listing details of a particular period such as local businesses, parks and amusement parks, prominent stores and shopping areas, and industries.

There is one more excellent source of background information. The interviewees themselves can provide source material by filling out specially prepared questionnaires relating to the interview topic prior to the interview. Copies of interviewees' biographical information, yearbooks, scrapbooks, photograph albums, and other items can aid in customizing interview questions as well.

KEYS FOR SUCCESS

Beyond focusing the topic, preparation of a written systematic plan, and thoughtful research, there are several other essential keys for a successful project worth repeating here. These include records control, clear job descriptions, effective recruitment of interviewees, and monitoring of each step in the project.

Retired textile worker Anne Murphy talks about her fellow workers and the managers at Newberger's towel factory in Paterson, New Jersey, at the end of World War I. Work and family photos, scrapbooks, letters, maps, and physical objects can serve as prompts or memory-joggers in an interview. *Courtesy of American Memory*

Control of record-keeping must be maintained for the interviews to have any lasting value as a collection or to be useful in a program or product. Proper filing and documentation must be maintained and are best handled by one person who is solely responsible for keeping the records. All materials, including the recordings, storage containers, and file folders must be clearly and consistently identified. Records of the project should be arranged in a rational order that will be useful to users. Transcriptions must be accurate and consistent, as described in chapter 6.

The successful implementation of the project depends upon clearly defined and understood job descriptions for the personnel performing various tasks. Generally, there should be one project director or coordinator who makes the assignments, keeps the records, does the correspondence, and assures the successful final disposition of the project. Next, there might be one or several interviewers, specifically trained to prepare, make contact, and conduct the interview with each interviewee, and

Simple Methods for Filing

1. Keep a separate file containing everything related to the interview (interview checklist, release, correspondence, original transcription, and other materials) for each interviewee. The simplest way to arrange such files is alphabetically by last name.

2. A database containing fields to cover each of the steps in the process of each interview is another good way to keep track of a project. The database must be monitored, kept up to date, and safely backed up on a separate server or hard drive. If a database is used, a unique automatic numbering system can be generated, but each interviewee number should be part of the paper file (as discussed in #1 above) as well.

3. Arrange files relating to the overall project in series by type, including: research materials; planning and budgeting information (proposals, records of board and committee actions, funding and budget details, schedules, etc.); interviewee recruitment lists; personnel recruitment and training materials; personnel records of those involved in the project; publicity materials; archives disposition records; and copyright and ownership materials.

4. Recorded interviews—whether they are audiotapes, videotapes, digital recordings, or some other medium—should be stored separately from the project files. The simplest arrangement is alphabetically by interviewee's last name (Smith, Don). Avoid mixing different media together because each type of recording has its own set of preservation needs and can actually be damaged by adjacent recordings if stored in the same container.

turn in the proper materials following the interview. After the interview is completed, the transcriber must handle each recording properly, assure the preservation of the original recording, and prepare consistent and accurate transcriptions. Also, if there is a separate equipment operator, whether video or audio, the operator must produce the best possible recording of the interview.

Another key to producing consistently effective interviews is to recruit and train a small number of skilled interviewers. Using a local volunteer recruiting agency is probably not the best way, as the agency is not as uniquely prepared as you are to select the best interviewer prospects. Using a formal written application and interview process, similar to the way museums recruit volunteer docents, is one effective way to assess prospective interviewers. Thorough training is crucial, and practice is the best learning experience for the interviewers once they have been recruited. Beware of prospective interviewers with previous experience as it may not prepare them for the oral history experience. Today's television interviewers sometimes seem to forget that the interview is not about the interviewer but about the interviewee. And a final word about using paid staff as interviewers: If they are conducting interviews, they probably are not performing the tasks central to their job descriptions—and this is the most expensive personnel cost of all.

A last and perhaps most important key for success is to identify the best interviewees for your project. Make use of the advisory committee's recommendations, carefully consider the scope of the project, and design publicity to attract the most desired interviewees. Most of the time, word-of-mouth references produce the most consistently good interviewees. Once the list of interviewees is made, attend to proper contact and follow-up; good communication with interviewees is the best advertisement of a quality project.

NOTES

1. Paul Richard Thompson, *The Voice of the Past: Oral History* (New York: Oxford University Press, 1978), 2.

Chapter Three

Ethics and Politics in Oral History Research

By Howard L. Sacks

When conducting oral history, you deliberately enter into another person's life. To say it more colloquially, oral history involves sticking your nose into other people's business. Questions of ethics and politics come into play in any human interaction but all the more so when you undertake a project intended for the general public. Before doing anything to implement a project, you must consider the ethical and political issues surrounding oral history research.

Two anecdotes illustrate the range of dilemmas one is likely to confront. A student of mine visited a local hog farmer to learn about his operation, the changes he's seen in agriculture, and his experiences living in a rural community. The interview went well; the student gathered a great deal of information, and the farmer enjoyed the opportunity to reflect on his daily work in response to the questions posed.

After the interview, the farmer asked the student if he'd like to stay for supper. Since home-cooked meals are a rare treat for college students, the student readily accepted. Not surprisingly, the main dish turned out to be pork. My student, a vegetarian, was faced with a dilemma. He didn't want to offend his host, who took pride in the food he raised. Indeed, he hoped to build a relationship with this farmer so that he might conduct further interviews. But eating meat violated his personal ethic. What was he to do?

The second story concerns a project on rural diversity. People in rural communities often assume that everyone around them thinks and believes pretty much as they do. Members of minority populations exist in nearly every town, but typically their numbers are small, so they don't challenge this assumption of homogeneity. One reason that rural dwellers find urban sprawl unappealing is its social consequences: New sorts of people enter the community, and this entails learning how to engage diversity.

To address this issue, my students conducted oral histories with individuals from various minority communities in our area. Irish Catholics were part of the region's frontier settlement. Belgians arrived more than a century ago to work in the glass factories. Hispanic migrants are more recent arrivals; some work as agricultural laborers. And several Indian physicians now have thriving practices in a range of specialties.

We approached a county newspaper with the idea of writing a series of essays on each of these communities. The editor was so delighted with the idea that she offered us twenty pages in the special magazine the newspaper publishes annually about the county's past and present. We gave the editor a list of the communities we had in mind, and she approved. Everyone was enthusiastic, and the students began their oral history work.

The essays were delivered to the newspaper on time, but a week before the publication date, we received a phone call from the agitated editor. When the paper's owner stopped by to look at the magazine's layout, she noticed that one of the essays was about the local gay and lesbian community. The owner objected vigorously and issued an ultimatum: Drop the essay or risk having the entire series canceled. This project represented a year's work for my students. In addition, we had told everyone in these communities that the essays would be published. What should we have done?

WHAT'S IN A NAME?

Words embed complex meanings and attitudes, so how we refer to those we interview carries implications for how we treat them. Market researchers and political pollsters usually refer to the people who answer their questions as *respondents.* That's an accurate description. People answering surveys are given limited choices: yes or no, agree or disagree, choose a point on a continuum between not important at all and very important, or choose from a list of product names or presidential primary contenders.

Traditionally, oral historians have called the people they interview *informants,* which acknowledges their primary role in providing information to a researcher. But it also minimizes their active role in shaping the narrative that constitutes the oral history, suggesting that they have little control over the questions asked or the use of the information. *Informant* also has the negative connotation of being associated with an informer—a usually anonymous informant who meets a police contact in a sleazy bar or a dark corner of a parking garage. That's not how we usually meet people who want to talk about quilts.

Then there's the super-sensitive and politically correct term *coresearcher,* a favorite in theses and dissertations. This term adequately captures the notion that the interview is a cooperative venture between two parties and that there is shared authority. But it suggests more. A true coresearcher would contribute to the design of the study, the methodology, and even the literature review. Despite well-intentioned attempts to seek community input in the selection of topics and questions, most researchers find that the people they want to interview lack the time, interest, or course background to really be involved as coresearchers.

We prefer the term *interviewee* (which complements the role of interviewer) or, alternatively, *narrator*. Both capture the spirit of shared authority in the interview and grant an active role to the person being interviewed. Because the term *narrator* carries many meanings and interpretations, for the sake of clarity we will use the term *interviewee* throughout this volume.

What we call someone or something is never neutral; all words come with values and connotations. Informants may supply valuable information, but the term suggests that they have little control over the questions asked or the use of the information. We prefer the term *interviewee,* which captures the spirit of shared authority in the interview and grants an active role to the person interviewed.

This debate over names may seem minor, but it calls attention to the important issue of power relationships in oral history research. In a recent project on farming techniques, my students interviewed an Amish family. The local Amish bishop gave us his permission for the interviews and even allowed us to tape record them. The results of this research were to be included on a Web site about farming and community life. But a few weeks before launching the project, the family members changed their minds and did not want us to use the interview material.

One can argue that as interviewees these individuals were treated ethically. The subject and purpose of the research were explained in detail, and they signed a release form giving the oral historian permission to use the materials in a public project. Thus, they lacked the power to determine what material was used from the interviews or how it was presented.

Interviewees may have a variety of reasons to limit or otherwise shape the information presented in an oral history project. For example, a farmer being interviewed in the mid-1990s explained his cutting-edge marketing techniques for selling commodities on the Internet; in this way, he avoided the brokers' fees charged for his products and reaped a higher profit. The farmer told the interviewer, "I'm willing to explain this to you, but I don't want you to publish this anywhere that other farmers can see it. It's my competitive advantage."

To what extent should interviewees define the use and presentation of the materials they provide? On the one hand, the information belongs to them; they are sharing their life experiences with you. At the same time, the understanding to be gained from this project typically transcends the perspective of any one individual you interview. The researcher hopes to create composite knowledge. Thus, participants must have a limited role in shaping the final project.

This issue manifests itself in a variety of decisions throughout the research process. What if an interviewee wants to place restrictions on the use of interview materials? Should individuals whose materials are used in the final project be allowed to review your selections prior to publication? Must interviewees have the opportunity to edit transcriptions of their comments before these documents enter a public archive?

SAFETY FIRST

Ethical issues apply not only to the interviewee but also to the interviewer. You must always be concerned with the well-being of those who conduct your project. Sites where interviews take place (farms or factories, for example) can be dangerous, particularly for individuals unfamiliar with the work routine. Anyone going alone to interview a stranger faces some risk. I always caution interviewers to leave a situation if they ever feel unsafe, regardless of how focused they are on completing their work.

Beyond concern over physical safety, interviewing can pose challenges to your personal integrity or well-being. Recall the vegetarian sitting down to a pork supper—not an unconflicted moment. Interviews also can sometimes involve emotionally troubling material. For example, a project documenting the Kent State University shootings on May 4, 1970, could stimulate the interviewer's own buried memories about traumatic experiences. But he or she might decide that it's worth rekindling painful emotions because the public deserves to learn more about that historical event. It helps to anticipate experiencing powerful emotions; it's not uncommon to lose sleep revisiting the details of another's difficult life story.

When interviewers come from a culture different from that of the community under study, they are apt to encounter values or attitudes that conflict with their own beliefs. This can have difficult repercussions for the interviewer. A Jewish interviewer who encounters anti-Semitism in the course of an interview but says nothing may be deeply troubled by not challenging such an offense.

> Interviewing can pose challenges to your personal integrity or well-being. For example, you may encounter values or attitudes that conflict with your own beliefs and thus have difficult repercussions for you.

SPEAKING FOR OTHERS

A few years ago I was dismayed to read an article in a major urban newspaper regarding the origins of the song "Dixie," which was the subject of a book I'd coauthored. Our thesis stated that the song, commonly attributed to Dan Emmett, a white minstrel from Knox County, Ohio, was in fact composed by a family of African American musicians with whom Emmett was acquainted. The columnist had read my book and subsequently called the local historical society museum for a response. The person he reached assured the writer that our thesis was untrue, and the museum staff had evidence to prove it.

Since my reputation as a professional scholar was at stake, I challenged the historical society to produce the evidence. As it turned out, the material was bogus. I chided the person who spoke to the newspaper writer for presenting her limited information as representative of the historical society's position on the matter. "Oh, you have that wrong," she replied. "I don't represent the historical society; I'm just a volunteer." I pointed out that when she answered the historical society's phone, the person on the other end of the line would quite appropriately take her to be an official of that organization.

A single individual rarely conducts a public oral history project. The project is typically sponsored by an organization—a church, historical society, corporation, or library. Everyone associated with that project thus serves as an ambassador for that sponsor in the community, and they must conduct themselves

A single individual rarely conducts a public oral history project. The project is typically sponsored by an organization—a church, historical society, corporation, or library. Everyone associated with the project serves as an ambassador for that sponsor in the community, and they must conduct themselves in a manner consistent with the image that organization wishes to present.

in a manner consistent with the image that organization wishes to present. Inappropriate action by a single interviewer can undermine not only the project's success but also the reputation of the organizations associated with it. It takes many achievements to build a positive reputation but just one misstep to ruin it.

Ethical conduct is particularly important to the institutions that fund or otherwise support your research. Funding agencies want to associate themselves with groups that have earned a positive reputation in their communities as well as a track record of successful projects. Taking care to inform everyone of appropriate standards of conduct in the course of the research thus has long-term implications for the groups organizing the effort.

GOING PUBLIC

The project that you fashion from your research—a film, exhibit, or book—presents a public image of those who contributed to it. How should you represent these individuals and the organization or community they represent?

Some of the dilemmas you'll face here are personal. An interviewee may find something he or she said embarrassing when it is shared with the public (it could be as simple as an ungrammatical word choice or a comment about a neighbor) or may think an old photograph is unflattering. Should you allow individuals to edit or veto material you wish to present publicly? Presumably, you explained the purpose of your research and the uses for the materials before conducting your interview. But is it worth the anger or hurt feelings that might be provoked by publicly presenting such material?

As with most ethical dilemmas in oral history research, the decision about what to present involves a judgment call. First and foremost, you must always ask how others are likely to interpret the materials you present. This may be particularly difficult; as a researcher, you may appreciate the nuances with which something was said, but these may be lost when you present a portion of that material out of context.

Clearly, those constructing the final presentation of your work must be sensitive to participants' preferences as well as the broader inclinations of the groups they represent. It is easier to discard questionable materials that are relatively peripheral to the central themes as opposed to those that make essential points. But beyond the logistical difficulties of allowing every participant to review a draft of your final project, you should be wary of giving participants too much editorial license. As previously noted, the story you choose to present from your research transcends any one participant's view. Indeed, there will be times when an individual's views stand in contrast to others' views or to your overall understanding of the events studied. When all is said and done, this is your project. You must be sensitive to those who provided you with information, but the responsibility for the final production rests with you.

The implications of what you present involve more than the individuals you interview. For example, a project on an ethnic group's experiences or a violent strike at a factory also reflects on the institutions or communities discussed. In our study of local black history, for example, we were concerned that simply bringing the black community into the public eye might compromise the invisibility that for many years had served as a strategy for avoiding prejudice and discrimination. You must be aware of your project's impact on the image and viability of those groups you represent. It may have been these concerns that motivated the newspaper owner to refrain from publishing an essay on the local gay community, as we discussed earlier. What would be the repercussions of such an essay for the newspaper and for the community's image? The issue this example raises is significant: How do we respect dominant community values while honestly representing a minority view?

Glossing over controversies to maintain a harmonious public image dilutes history and is rarely satisfying. Editing out sensitive material often does a disservice to those who granted you interviews in the hope that their story would be told. But when the project is over, everyone involved has to live together.

Of course, projects are sometimes most powerful when they stimulate public discussion by challenging persisting attitudes. Glossing over controversies to maintain a harmonious public image dilutes history and is rarely satisfying. Editing out sensitive material often does a disservice to those who granted you interviews in the hope that their story would be told. But when the project is over, everyone involved has to live together. And if you conduct work in a community other than your own, remember that *you* leave, but they stay; the work can have long-term impact on real, ongoing lives.

SOME GUIDELINES

Oral history involves face-to-face interaction, and therefore circumstances will be unique and not perfectly predictable. Discussing the ethics and politics associated with your research at the outset with everyone working on the project will not provide a solution to every imaginable dilemma, but it will sensitize them to this dimension of the work. That way, when a snap judgment is required, project members are less likely to be taken aback by the situation and to make an unreasoned decision.

It's impossible to establish a hard-and-fast set of rules for dealing with all sensitive situations. However, we can establish general guidelines that will help you avoid many problems and deal effectively with those you do confront.

Follow the Golden Rule

Empathy is fundamental to all communication, and it serves you particularly well in anticipating and avoiding ethical problems. Ask yourself how you would feel if someone treated you as you are about to treat another. If the answer is "not so good," then another course of action is probably called for.

When in Rome, Do as the Romans Do

When you conduct oral history research, you enter into the world of others. As a guest in their home, workplace, or com-

A Sunday religious gathering at the home of an Amish family in central Ohio. Mindful of prohibitions against photographing the Amish, the photographer took care to capture collective life without including individuals in the picture. Interviewers and researchers should respect cultural traditions. *Courtesy of Howard L. Sacks*

munity, you should respect their values and rules of conduct. For example, the rural community surrounding Kenyon College is generally religious and conservative. So I tell my students to dress appropriately and keep politically or sexually provocative apparel at home.

It is crucial to remember that you are there to observe and collect information, not to judge. It is almost never appropriate for you to comment upon or challenge an interviewee's position, even if you find the person's views personally offensive. Sometimes it's not easy. In our project documenting local black history, one of my students began an interview with a local school official by describing the purpose of our research. The official asked, "Why would you be interested in something as insignificant as that?" His comment was doubly offensive. As an educator, he should have been more supportive of a student project. And the student interviewing him was an

African American from the local community who had attended his school.

Of course, deciding which community standards to follow can pose its own complexities. Even in a single institution or rural community, diverse viewpoints abound. In Knox County, for example, the values of students at Kenyon College differ significantly from those of students at Mount Vernon Nazarene University, located just a few miles down the road. The worldviews of the local black and Amish communities are, in some respects, quite different from those of the dominant community. Kenyon's faculty is largely cosmopolitan in background, while most staff members have lived their entire lives in the immediate locale. Doing fieldwork thus involves repeated acts of cultural translation. Never assume that those you interview necessarily subscribe to your values; when values conflict, keep your opinions to yourself.

Honesty Is the Best Policy

Oral history is valuable and important, but it doesn't rise to the level of undercover intelligence work. Never misrepresent yourself or your project in the hope of getting better material. Transparency is the rule here. If you are clear in stating what you want and why, you're unlikely to find yourself confronted by an ethical dilemma in the course of your research.

Bear in mind, however, that being honest about what you're doing can go too far. In introducing their work, for example, graduate students often burden their would-be interviewees with overly complex explanations of the thesis underlying their research, the theoretical underpinnings of their ideas, and the empirical model that will guide the effort. In the same vein, don't offer your potential interviewees more information than is needed to explain the project and their role in it. Instead, provide them with sufficient information about the project to make an informed decision about whether or not to participate. A release form, which we'll discuss further on in chapter 4, can be valuable by providing a clear and concise statement of the purpose and uses of your research. Of course, you should allow participants to ask additional questions about your project.

Do What You Promise to Do

Like many of these guidelines, doing what you promise to do is easier said than done. For example, it would be inconsiderate to arrive late for a scheduled interview. But arriving on time, particularly in a strange neighborhood, requires planning and effort. Obtain clear directions, allow extra time for traffic or parking, and make sure you have change for the meter. Acting responsibly often means paying close attention to seemingly insignificant details; that's something not everyone does by nature.

It's not uncommon or unreasonable for interviewees to make requests of you during your visit. They may ask you for a copy of the interview tape to share with family members. If you obtain an old photograph to reproduce, they may ask for a copy

An interviewer gives her interviewees an album of family photos she took as part of her research. An interview is always a transaction, and this is one way of giving something back to individuals who have shared their time and memories. *Courtesy of the Rural Life Center, Kenyon College*

These guidelines will enable you to avoid many problems and deal effectively with those you do confront.

- Empathy is fundamental to all communications, and it serves you particularly well in anticipating and avoiding ethical problems.
- You are there to observe and collect information, not to judge.
- Never misrepresent yourself or the project in the hope of getting better material.
- Always do what you promise to do.
- Focus interviews on what you want to know; avoid straying from the subject of the project.
- Involve individuals from the community under study in every phase of your project.

of that, too. Because you want to establish good rapport and believe that it's morally right to reciprocate in this way for their time, you're likely to readily agree to such requests. But it takes time and effort to reproduce and deliver materials, and too often these promises go unfulfilled in the rush of a public research project. Breaking your promise casts an unflattering light on you, your project, and the organizations associated with it. And the next researcher to come along will certainly receive a chilly reception.

Focus Your Interviews on What You Want to Know

The less your interview strays from the subject of the project, the more likely you are to avoid subject areas that may make interviewees uncomfortable or pose ethical dilemmas. In chapter 5, we'll discuss the crucial importance of follow-up questions that enable you to explore something an interviewee says more deeply. The point here is that it may be best not to follow up on something said in passing that isn't germane to your primary interest. For example, in an interview on a local glassblowing industry, your subject may tell you that he got a job at a local plant following his service in World War II. The relevance of his military duty to your subject is not readily apparent, and asking about it could bring back painful memories that would only hamper your interview or bog it down in detail you don't truly wish to explore.

At the same time, sometimes the best material in an interview arises from a train of thought that initially appears to be tangential to the subject at hand. Perhaps this veteran saw action in Italy and took up glassblowing because of a chance encounter with a local artisan he met while on leave. That would be a wonderful story—one you would have missed had you decided that the war was too sensitive or too peripheral to pursue. Oral history involves a series of decisions, often between competing goods.

Democratize Your Research

The importance of this cannot be overstated. By involving individuals from the community under study in every phase of your project, you can avoid many of the problems that otherwise can besiege oral history work. People familiar with the community can tell you if certain topics are taboo, whether it's inappropriate to call people's homes at certain times, or how to conduct yourself in particular ways when visiting a church or fraternal organization. Getting feedback from insiders who understand your project can also help you avoid making gaffes in your public presentation that might cause hurt feelings or conflicts. Beyond the value of democratization in avoiding ethical and political dilemmas, involving community members will contribute to a richer research effort and an enthusiastic public reception.

Chapter Four

Legal Issues

By David H. Mould

You're interviewing the former mayor of your city about his career as a public servant. It's a lively session. The mayor has a treasure trove of stories about past political battles and intrigues. You ask for his opinion of the current mayor who defeated him in the last election. He doesn't hold back. "That morally delinquent deadbeat? He's just a sneaky, groveling office-seeker, a con man who buys votes, sells influence, and swindles the taxpayers. He serves the Mafia, not the people."

This is terrific stuff, but you'll be wise not to use it in your public program or radio series on the city's history. The ex-mayor may have legitimate concerns about the conduct of the last election—especially those unopened ballot boxes discovered six weeks later at the city dump—but he is making a libelous statement. Indeed, in three sentences, I've used nine red-flag words listed by libel expert Bruce Sanford. The list of words and expressions in Sanford's *Libel and Privacy* is gleaned from actual cases.[1] None of these words used alone will trigger a libel suit; that depends on the context and the person named. But it pays to be careful.

What's the problem? You didn't use the red-flag words; the ex-mayor did. Surely, he's responsible for what he says. In fact, you are both responsible, and so is your organization. The ex-mayor used the words, but you published them and brought the libelous statement to the public.

Oral historians are less likely than journalists, photographers, plastic surgeons, and used car dealers to be sued. But there have been court cases involving the content of oral history interviews and legal disputes over the ownership and use of interviews. At universities, institutional review boards (IRBs) have attempted to place restrictions on interviewing. Oral historians need to follow basic guidelines to stay out of trouble and to be aware of developing case law.

The purpose of this chapter is not to provide a comprehensive review of state and federal statutes and cases or to summarize all legal issues that an oral historian could face. For the past twenty-five years, these tasks have been diligently and masterfully performed by historian and judge John Neuenschwander in *Oral History and the Law.*[2] Nor is the purpose of this chapter to dispense legal advice. That's what lawyers do. So if you have a specific problem or question, consult an attorney. However, this chapter will provide an overview of legal issues and guidelines to help you stay out of trouble. We'll start with that bankrupt, blacklisted, corrupt, cowardly, hypocritical (five more words from Sanford's list) thing called defamation.

DEFAMATION

The good news is that I can't be sued for publishing that last sentence. In the United States, only an individual person or an organization can sue for libel. Words, ideologies, countries, professions, domestic pets, and inanimate objects can't. As a native Briton, I'm sometimes offended by American stereotypes of what it means to be British—some combination of binge tea drinking, gardening, hunting foxes, doting on the royal family, and living in a stone cottage in a village called Middle-Wallup-under-the-Wolds. But I can't sue a travel magazine for an article that idealizes rural Britain because there's no way to prove that the bucolic portrayal has injured my personal reputation. Similarly, as a university professor, I don't think I live in an ivory tower, but I can't sue critics who believe academe is out of touch with the world.

However, a corporation, religious group, labor union, or nonprofit organization can sue for defamation if it can prove that damage was done to its collective reputation and not to its individual staff or representatives. In business, where the value of a brand and customer goodwill may be a company's greatest assets, this provides protection against unfounded claims by competitors or disgruntled customers. In the nonprofit sector, where trust and transparency are key currencies, a faith-based or charitable organization may sue if it is accused of misuse of funds on the grounds that such accusations reduce public trust and contributions.

The issue of group and individual identification becomes difficult in smaller communities. There's no problem with the statement "All politicians are crooks," or even "All politicians in the state are crooks." But if your interviewee states, "All members of the city council recycling committee are hypocrites because they throw aluminum cans in their trash," and the committee has only six members, they are easily identifiable. It's a matter of scale; a phrase that would cause offense (but not a lawsuit) in a large city may be considered defamatory in a smaller community. It's also a matter of time. Most states require a plaintiff to sue within one year of the first publication of defamatory material. The purpose of the statute of limitations is to prevent people from dredging up old offenses to settle new scores and to prevent frivolous suits by cranks and professional litigants.

It's often said that we should not speak ill of the dead. However, there's no law against it. If the mayor of our fictitious city files a libel suit against you, your organization, and the ex-mayor but then dies from a blow to the head with a tape recorder, you may be questioned in the criminal matter, but the suit will die with the plaintiff. This limitation provides a measure of protection for oral history programs because, as Neuenschwander wryly notes, interviewees "are often recounting events involving participants who have long since gone off to their graves."[3]

Defamation is a false statement that injures the reputation of another. Words that may injure a person's reputation are classified into five categories:

1. committing a crime
2. acting immorally or unethically
3. associating with unsavory people or otherwise acting disgracefully or despicably
4. demonstrating financial irresponsibility or unreliability
5. demonstrating professional incompetency[4]

A written defamatory statement is called libel; a spoken defamatory statement is called slander. The courts have viewed slander as a less serious offense because the utterance is usually spontaneous. Libel is more serious because the act of writing is considered deliberate. This places the oral history interview in a somewhat ambiguous legal position. Defamatory words, at the time of utterance, are slander. But recording and publishing them—in a book, exhibition, or documentary—are clearly deliberate and not spontaneous actions, so defamation in interviews is generally considered libel.

A plaintiff needs to prove five elements to establish a claim for defamation:

1. The words used were defamatory.
2. The defamation was about the plaintiff.
3. The defamation was published to a third person.
4. The plaintiff's reputation was damaged.
5. The defendant was somehow at fault.

An oral history organization cannot dodge responsibility by using phrases such as "it is alleged" or "so-and-so claims." It has

Bruce Sanford's Red-Flag Words and Phrases

addict
adulteration of products
adultery
AIDS
alcoholic
altered records
atheist
bad moral character
bankrupt
bigamist
blacklisted
blackmail
boozehound
bribery
brothel
buys votes
cheats
child abuse
collusion
con artist
confidence man
corruption
coward
crook
deadbeat
defaulter
divorced
double-crosser
drug abuser
drunkard
ex-convict
fawning sycophant
fraud
gambling den
gangster
gay
graft
groveling office-seeker
herpes
hit man
hypocrite
illegitimate
illicit relation
incompetent
infidelity
informer
insider trading
intemperate
intimate
intolerance
Jekyll-Hyde personality
kept woman
Ku Klux Klan
Mafia
mental illness
mobster
moral delinquency
mouthpiece
Nazi
paramour
Peeping Tom
perjurer
plagiarist
pockets public funds
profiteering
prostitute
rape
rapist
scam
scandalmonger
scoundrel
seducer
sharp dealing
shyster
slacker
smooth and tricky
smuggler
sneaky
sold influence
sold out
spy
stool pigeon
stuffed the ballot box
suicide
swindle
thief
unethical
unmarried mother
unprofessional
unsound mind
unworthy of credit
vice den
villain

Source: Bruce Sanford, *Libel and Privacy* (New York: Aspen Law and Business, 1991), 4.13.

republished the defamation and is legally liable along with the interviewee.

Most libel cases in the United States in the last fifty years have involved journalists or authors and their organizations—newspapers, broadcasting companies, and book publishers. There are so many similarities between how oral historians use interviews—in public programs, museum exhibits, articles, books, radio and television programs, and Web sites—and how journalists and authors use interviews, that it is clear that the courts will apply the same standards developed in earlier case law.

Your organization can be held liable for words an interviewee utters, assuming they are repeated, published, or redistributed. Strictly speaking, the size of the audience is not the issue, although this will likely make a difference in damages awarded; a judge will be tougher on a TV network that reaches millions of viewers than on the publisher of a community newsletter. The test is whether there was an intelligible communication to a third party. This means that, at least in principle, you are not protected from a libel suit by leaving the offending interview tape on a shelf in the archive and not using it in a public program. If a visiting researcher listens to the interview, communication has occurred. And if the researcher publishes the quote, all parties can be held liable. The main exception to the "you're-as-guilty-as-the-interviewee" principle applies to Web sites that host the posts of third-party users. Under section 230 of the Communications Decency Act of 1996, these sites are provided broad immunity to defamation and tort liability. In other words, the person defamed can sue the individual who made the post but not the organization that sponsors the Web site.

One key doctrine of libel law is that public officials and public figures, such as sports and entertainment celebrities, have voluntarily placed themselves in the public eye and should expect a certain degree of scrutiny and criticism. To prove libel, a public official or public figure must show that the statement was made with *actual malice*. A private individual, by contrast, deserves more protection and simply has to show that negligence occurred. The so-called *public official standard* was established in the landmark *New York Times v. Sullivan* case in 1964, when the police commissioner of Montgomery, Alabama, sued over an advertisement paid for by civil rights activists that claimed public officials had acted unfairly and illegally in dealing with nonviolent black protestors. The Supreme Court overturned an Alabama Supreme Court decision and damages award on the grounds that constitutional guarantees of freedom of speech would be limited if public officials were allowed to sue for any erroneous statement. To prove libel, the plaintiff had to show actual malice—that the defendant knew the statement was false or acted with reckless disregard for the truth. In 1974, the decision in *Gertz v. Robert Welch, Inc.*, extended the actual malice standard to public figures, and established a simple negligence standard for private individuals. In determining whether someone is a public figure, a court needs to decide whether a controversy exists and the nature and the extent of the person's involvement in the controversy.

The interpretation of the public official and public figure standards has been a contentious issue. Clearly, the former mayor in our example is still considered a public official, and former entertainment and sports stars who use their celebrity status to further their careers are public figures. What about a private individual who has a brief moment in the public spotlight as an advocate for a cause or because of a heroic act or a notorious crime? This is the so-called *vortex public figure*, known only in connection with a single issue or controversy. In *Street v. National Broadcasting Company* (1981), a case brought by the state's chief witness in the famous 1933 Scottsboro Boys trials over how she was portrayed in a TV dramatization of the trials, the U.S. Court of Appeals for the Sixth Circuit held, "[O]nce a person becomes a public figure in connection with the particular controversy, that person remains a public figure thereafter for purposes of later commentary or treatment of that controversy." In other words, once a public figure, always a public figure, but only in connection with a specific controversy. If the libelous statement concerns a different issue, the plaintiff will be considered a private individual and will have to show only simple negligence. However, this may not be the final word on the issue. Although other circuit courts support the position of the Sixth, the U.S. Supreme Court has yet to take a case that tests this definition.

There's one watertight defense against libel, and that's truth. If you can show that the statement—however much it may have injured a reputation—is true, then the plaintiff has no case. Some statements are also protected by privilege. Legislators speaking in debates on the floor of Congress or most state legislatures cannot be sued for defamation. However, they cannot take privilege with them once they leave the chamber, so interviews do not enjoy the protection. The expression of an opinion—the so-called *fair comment standard*—is also a defense. If it wasn't, editorial writers could not do their jobs, restaurant and theater critics would give only glowing reviews, and advocacy groups would live in fear of legal reprisal.

The number of libel suits has been steadily increasing, and this trend will likely continue with the expansion of the Internet. With the popularity of blogging, online video postings, and increased interactivity, the potential for libelous statements is greater than ever. Oral history projects need to monitor their Web sites, not only for the transcripts and audio and video clips they post but also for the comments and feedback they receive from users and for threaded online discussions.[5]

So what do you do when you come across a potentially defamatory statement? Neuenschwander recommends cutting out the defamatory words or deleting the identity of the person being attacked during the editing process. As a last resort, a portion of the interview can be sealed.

One final caveat: This discussion of libel law applies only to the United States. Other countries have tougher libel laws. In some countries in the developing world, impugning the honor and dignity of a public official is enough to land you in court and (where libel is still a criminal offense) maybe in jail. Truth or fair comment are no defenses in societies in which the law specifically protects family name and honor. If you're intending to collect or publish oral history interviews in another country, you need to check which laws apply.

RELEASE FORMS AND COPYRIGHT

The interview, like a newspaper, magazine, book, film, painting, or sculpture, is intellectual property. That means it can be bought, sold, licensed, or left in a will to heirs. Over the years, some historical documents have turned up on the auction block at Sotheby's or Christie's. Some oral history interviews, such as those with former U.S. presidents, may have cash value, but museums and archives don't usually sell them off. Your county historical society isn't going to make much money advertising its interviews in the classifieds or on eBay. Most interviews are simply given away. But to establish ownership, this must be a legal transaction.

Most oral history programs use a standardized release form, signed by both interviewee and interviewer. Our sample is designed to be clear and comprehensive, yet flexible. Legally, a release consists of two parts—a deed of gift or contract and an assignment of copyright. It is important to separate these two rights. An interviewee may donate the physical recording of an interview to an archive but retain some (or all) literary property rights. Politicians, entertainers, and sports stars are understandably reluctant to give up rights to interviews they may want to use when they write books about their careers; if they sign away copyright now, they will need to ask permission later to use their own quotes. More commonly, an interviewee may grant some rights but not others, for example, allowing the program to make the interview available to researchers but not licensing it for commercial use.

Because most oral history programs are nonprofit, the deed of gift, defined as the voluntary transfer of property without consideration, is more commonly used than the contract.[6] To be considered a gift, both interviewee and interviewer must agree to conduct the interview and donate it, and the interview must be delivered to and accepted by the sponsoring organization. A simple sentence, such as "I hereby give, convey, and assign my interview recorded on (date) to the (oral history organization) as a donation," is sufficient.

The second part is the assignment of copyright. In the United States, interviews, like other types of intellectual property, are governed by the Copyright Act of 1976.[7] This law replaced a 1909 statute, whose provisions had long been regarded as out of date because they did not address the ownership issues raised by radio and television. The Copyright Act requires that any transfer of copyright ownership must be in writing and signed by the rights holder. Again, this can be accomplished with a simple sentence such as "I hereby assign legal title and all literary property rights, including copyright, in my interview recorded on (date) to the (project)."

According to the Copyright Act, copyright protection exists for "original works of authorship fixed in any tangible medium of expression." A tape, cassette, disk, or digital storage device is a tangible medium of expression. Once the interview has ended and the recording device is switched off, an original work has been created. Although the interviewee has done most of the talking, the work can be considered a joint creation by the interviewee and interviewer. The notion of shared authority (discussed in chapter 5) is not simply a theoretical construct. The Copyright Act defines a joint work as "a work prepared by two or more authors with the intention that their contributions be merged into inseparable or interdependent parts of a unitary whole." Although there has been no court ruling on this issue, the U.S. Copyright Office defines the interview as a joint work containing "copyrightable authorship by the person interviewed and the interviewer. Each owns the expression in the absence of an agreement to the contrary." That's why it's important for both interviewee and interviewer to sign the release form.[8]

If the interviewer is an employee of the organization sponsoring the project, the contribution is considered *work made for hire*. This means that—unless there is a specific agreement granting rights to the interviewer—copyright belongs to the organization; the interviewer has no rights and does not need to sign the release. Many oral history programs, however, rely on freelance, part-time, or volunteer interviewers. Because they are not employees but independent contractors (even if unpaid), they should sign the release, thus assigning copyright to the organization.

Some novice interviewers are reluctant to use releases. They think that the interviewee may feel intimidated by having to sign a legal form and that the quality of the interview will suffer. Neuenschwander considers such fears exaggerated. Almost everyone, he points out, has had some contact with legal documents—from a mortgage to a credit card application to a speeding ticket. The interviewer needs to explain that a signed release form is required in order for the interview to be transcribed, edited, cataloged, preserved, and used in a public program.[9]

Many interviewers go over the release form before the interview begins and ask the interviewee to sign it. It's certainly convenient to deal with the pesky paperwork up front, and most interviewees willingly sign the form. Strictly speaking, however, no transfer of intellectual property has been made; the interview has not yet begun, and no work of authorship has been created. This matter of timing may seem a legal nicety; indeed, I know of no cases in which oral historians have had to testify in court as to the precise time when the interviewee signed the form. But it's a point worth considering. Legally, you can't give away something that doesn't yet exist. And technically that's what is happening when an interviewee signs a release form before the interview begins.

What kind of information should go into the release? Each organization needs to develop a standardized form that meets its own objectives. An archive that collects interviews primarily for use by academic researchers and puts on the occasional public program will need one kind of form; a project that plans to produce radio and television documentaries, adapt interview transcripts into dramatic scripts, and publish extended excerpts on its Web site will need another. Of course, it's difficult to predict future uses for oral history interviews. Those long-forgotten tapes on farm life in the 1940s may be discovered by a TV documentary producer. However, the releases the interviewees signed twenty years ago stated that they would be used for research and an exhibit at the local library. What do you do? Legally, you should go back to each interviewee and ask for a new release granting new rights—or insist that the documentary producer do so. This may be difficult. Interviewees move away, get cranky in their old age, and sometimes die. The key to avoiding this problem is to draft an all-purpose release form that grants the organization flexibility in determining future uses of the interview.

Our sample release form begins with a brief description of the project and a statement that the recordings and transcripts will be deposited in the oral history organization's collection and "made available for historical research and public dissemination." It states that participation in the project is voluntary. Both interviewee and interviewer voluntarily donate to the organization "full use of the information contained in the recordings made on [date], transcripts of these recordings, and other materials collected." It is essential to specify transcripts because a transcript, a written version of the interview, is not

Sample Release Form

The ______________ oral history project (project) is a program of the [organization name]. Recordings and transcripts resulting from interviews conducted for the project will be deposited in the oral history collection of [organization name], where they will be made available for historical research and public dissemination. Participation in the project is entirely voluntary.

I, the undersigned, have read the above and voluntarily donate to the project full use of the information contained in the recordings made on ______________ (date), transcripts of the recordings, and other materials collected during the interview.

I hereby assign legal title and all literary property rights, including copyright, in these recordings and transcripts to the project, which may copyright and publish said materials. The information may be used for scholarly or educational purposes as determined by the project (except as noted below).

Restrictions on use:____

____

____

______________________________ Interviewee's signature Date	______________________________ Interviewer's signature Date
______________________________ Interviewee's name (please print clearly)	______________________________ Interviewer's name (please print clearly)
Interviewee's address:	Interviewer's address:
Street ____________________	Street ____________________
City ________ State____ Zip____	City ________ State___ Zip_____

If interviewee is minor, signature of parent or guardian:

____

Signature Date

the same as the original recording; under the Copyright Act, it is classified as a *derivative work.* Including "other materials" allows the use of photographs, written documents, or other materials collected at the interview.

The release goes on to state that the information (from recordings and transcripts) "may be used for scholarly or educational purposes" as determined by the organization. This gives you freedom in deciding how the interviews will be used in the future; you will not have to obtain new release forms anytime someone wants to use the interviews in a project. Of course, if you know precisely how the interviews will be used—for a museum exhibit, with a Web site and a DVD and study guide for local schools—then you can specify these uses. However, it's still a good idea to include language that allows other potential uses, including publication on the Internet.

Copyright to an interview gives the organization five exclusive rights:

1. to reproduce the interview, i.e., to make copies
2. to make derivative works, including the transcript, print or Web-based articles, and audio and video programs
3. to distribute copies by sale, rental, lease, and lending
4. to perform the work publicly (including digital audio Web streaming for sound recordings)
5. to display the work publicly[10]

These rights are essentially separate. This means that if you sell a copy of the interview tape, the buyer can play it for personal use but does not have the right to use it at a public forum, put it on a Web site, or edit it into an audio or video documentary. Essentially, copyright law allows you to divide up the rights in any number of ways. For example, you may grant the right to copy and publish an interview (either exclusively or nonexclusively) but grant no right to make derivative works.

An excellent guide to the range of options in copyright licensing is provided by Creative Commons (CC), a nonprofit organization that provides a free online service to help authors, scientists, and educators license their work. With a CC license, you keep your copyright but allow people to copy and distribute your work with attribution and under certain conditions. In the United States, CC offers six types of licenses:

1. Attribution 3.0: You allow others to copy, distribute, display, and perform your work, and make derivative works from it, but only if they give you credit in the way you specify.
2. Attribution-Noncommercial 3.0: You grant the same rights as in License #1 but on condition that the work is not used for commercial purposes.
3. Attribution-Noncommercial-No Derivative Works 3.0: You grant the same rights as in License #2 but with the provision that your work cannot be changed or edited.
4. Attribution-Noncommercial-Share Alike 3.0: You grant the right to make noncommercial derivative works on condition that they are licensed in the same way as the original.
5. Attribution-No Derivative Works 3.0: You allow others to copy, distribute, display, and perform your work but not to make derivative works.
6. Attribution-Share Alike 3.0: You grant the right to make derivative works (including those for commercial use) on condition that they are licensed in the same way as the original.[11]

Oral history organizations that post interview excerpts or transcripts on Web sites may find the licenses useful. They should include a Some Rights Reserved button linking back to CC. Licenses are provided in three formats: a commons deed, a simple, plain-language summary of the license; legal code, the fine print to make sure the license will stand up in court; and digital code, a machine-readable translation of the license that helps search engines and other applications identify the work by its terms of use.

Under the fair use provision of the Copyright Act, others are allowed to use portions of a copyrighted work without permission from the owner. The act contains four standards that courts are to apply whenever fair use is raised as a defense to a suit for copyright infringement:

1. the purpose and character of the use, including whether such use is of a commercial nature or is for nonprofit educational purposes
2. the nature of the copyrighted work
3. the amount and substantiality of the portion used in relation to the copyrighted work as a whole
4. the effect of the use upon the potential market for or value of the copyrighted work[12]

Under these guidelines, using a two- to three-minute excerpt from a one-hour interview is fair use. Using a fifteen- or twenty-minute excerpt poses a more difficult question because it involves a substantial portion of the work. However, if it is being used for nonprofit educational purposes and for a limited time, it could be considered fair use. In the absence of clear guidelines from the courts, many libraries, universities, schools, and other nonprofit institutions have adopted their own fair use rules.

Some release forms include an indemnity clause protecting the organization from legal liability arising out of use of the interviews. There is debate among oral historians about whether it's ethical to hold the interviewee responsible for any legal action that could arise. Neuenschwander considers an indemnity clause "totally out of sync" with the spirit of mutual trust and social responsibility that should guide oral history projects.[13]

However, some programs, usually on the advice of an attorney, include such a clause. Here's some sample wording: "I release the (oral history organization), its participants, and others acting under its authority from any liability or claim of liability concerning the use of these recordings, transcripts, and materials, including but not limited to, any claims for defamation, invasion of privacy, or right of publicity." Publishers and media organizations insist on this kind of provision to protect themselves from lawsuits for copyright infringement and libel. In recent years, well-known historians have been accused of plagiarism or at least of quoting long passages without attribution. If the interview is libelous, this language will probably not save you from a lawsuit, but it may reduce the damages awarded.

Finally, the interviewee and interviewer "assign legal title and all literary property rights, including copyright, in the [scholarly materials] to the [oral history organization], which may copyright and publish said materials." Interviewee and interviewer sign and date their agreement and add their contact information. If the interviewee is a minor, a parent or guardian must sign the release.

The release form should include a section in which the interviewee can set restrictions on use or seal the interview by placing a time embargo on its release. It is quite reasonable for an interviewee to agree to use by researchers and for public programs but not for other uses. If there's a prospect that the interview will end up in a book on the *New York Times* best-seller list or inspire a script for a Hollywood blockbuster, then the interviewee has a right to ask for a new release. Public officials and politicians who talk about their careers and political enemies, past and present, sometimes insist on an embargo. They are understandably concerned that the release of the interview will be embarrassing to others and may even hurt their own political prospects, so they request that the interview be sealed for a specified number of years or until after their death.

Sometimes, an interviewee may request that portions of the recording or transcript be deleted. Do not automatically agree to such a request. After all, the interviewee agreed to do the interview and perhaps should not have said something he or she would later regret. However, if you need to agree to the request (usually because the alternative is not obtaining a release), then document the change in the transcript with a note that states, "Removed at the request of the interviewee" or "Edited by the interviewee."

Under the 1976 Copyright Act, copyright exists from the moment the work is created. Unlike the old 1909 act, which stated that copyright had to be registered to establish ownership, the current law protects unregistered and unpublished works as well. This is another good reason to label the tape and box with the recording date and (because labels peel off) record the date along with other identifying information (see chapter 9). Once the interview is ready for public use, a copyright symbol should be conspicuously placed on the tape and box. This is about as far as most oral history programs go in establishing copyright given the time and expense involved in registration. However, registering a work with the Copyright Office at the Library of Congress is required before a copyright holder can file a lawsuit for alleged infringement. If you have the only interview ever recorded with the person who claims to have seen the Loch Ness Monster surfacing in Lake Erie, it's definitely worth registering. The Copyright Office Web site contains circulars and forms, including the useful *Copyright Basics* and Form TX (for a nondramatic literary work) that is used to register all audio and video interviews and transcripts for a fee.[14] Most programs cannot afford to register individual interviews. Fortunately, the Copyright Office allows the registration of unpublished works as a collection. Because most interviews are part of a broader project and are collected over a period of months or years, the best option is to register the interviews or transcripts as a collection with a single title.

An archive or program that holds the recordings or transcripts of interviews does not own them if there are no legal releases. If the interviewee has died, the program should try to track down the legal heirs and secure a release. Another option is to have the interviewer sign a release. Because the Copyright Office considers interviewers as joint authors, it allows them to convey a nonexclusive license to use the interview without approval. If all attempts to secure release forms fail, the program will have to decide what use to allow (if any) and realize that any use is technically a breach of copyright. This has led some archives to interpret the rules strictly; some permit access to such interviews but do not allow quotation or copying of the transcript or tape.

Because of changes in the copyright law, you need to check specific copyright terms, especially for works created or published between 1978 and 2002. The most comprehensive guide is Peter Hirtle's annually updated "Copyright Term and the Public Domain in the United States."[15]

If neither your organization nor the interviewee has any interest in protecting copyright, and you want to make the interview as widely available as possible, then why start by restricting use? Your legal release can simply state that the interview will be in the public domain, available to anyone. Creative Commons provides a public domain dedication license, valid for the United States. Putting your interviews in the public domain involves giving up all rights. Others can copy, sell, and make derivative works from the interviews without permission or acknowledgement. The work may be "exploited by anyone for any purpose, commercial or non-commercial, and in any way, including by methods that have not yet been invented or conceived."[16] You should read that last sentence again before you surrender rights and decide to put your organization's interviews in the public domain.

SEALING INTERVIEWS

An interviewee may request that the interview—or portions of it—be sealed for a number of years. Politicians and public

United States Terms of Copyright	
Unpublished work	Life of the author plus 70 years
Unpublished anonymous work or work for hire	120 years from date of creation
Unpublished work created before 1978, published after 1977 but before 2003	Life of the author plus 70 years or December 31, 2047, whichever is greater
Unpublished work created before 1978, published after 2002	Life of the author plus 70 years
Unpublished work where the date of author's death is not known	120 years from date of creation
Work published before 1923	In the public domain
Work published between 1923 and 1977 without copyright notice	In the public domain
Work published between 1923 and 1963 with copyright notice, but the copyright has not been renewed	In the public domain
Work published between 1923 and 1963 with copyright notice, which was renewed	95 years after publication date
Work published between 1978 and March 1, 1989, without copyright notice and without subsequent registration within 5 years	In the public domain
Work published between 1978 and March 1, 1989, without copyright notice but with subsequent registration within 5 years	Life of the author plus 70 years or, if work for hire, 95 years from publication
Work created after 1977 and published between 1978 and March 1, 1989, with copyright notice	Life of the author plus 70 years or, if work for hire, 95 years from publication
Work created before 1978 and published between 1978 and March 1, 1989, with copyright notice	Life of the author plus 70 years or, if work for hire, 95 years from publication or December 31, 2047, whichever is greater
Work created after 1977 and published between March 1, 1989, and 2002	Life of the author plus 70 years or, if work for hire, 95 years from publication
Work created before 1978 and published between March 1, 1989, and 2002	Life of the author plus 70 years or, if work for hire, 95 years from publication or December 31, 2047, whichever is greater
Work published after 2002	Life of the author plus 70 years or, if work for hire, 95 years from publication

Adapted from Peter Hirtle, "Copyright Term and the Public Domain in the United States," *Cornell Copyright Information Center,* http://www.copyright.cornell.edu/public_domain/.

figures who talk about contemporary events and people are most likely to seek such restrictions so that they can speak frankly without fear of retribution or a libel suit. An interviewee may also request anonymity; an illegal immigrant, an opposition leader in exile, a corporate whistleblower, or a former crime boss have more than a reputation to protect—often, lives are at stake.

Oral history programs need to document restrictions listed on release forms and make sure their staff members understand them. Releasing a sealed portion of an interview or transcript or ignoring a time embargo on publication may result in a lawsuit. However, restrictions listed on a release form will likely not stand up in a criminal or civil court case in which lawyers want to introduce the interviews as evidence. Neuenschwander recommends that any undertaking to bar or restrict access should be qualified by a statement that the agreement may not be legally enforceable if a valid subpoena is issued.[17]

Litigants routinely seek historical records to use as evidence. In *Wilkinson v. F.B.I.* (1986), the FBI sought access to sealed papers held at the State Historical Society of Wisconsin, arguing that they were essential to its defense against a civil rights action. The district court refused to recognize the agreement protecting the sealed papers from discovery. In the 1998 trial of Ku Klux Klan leader Samuel H. Bowers for the murder of a civil rights leader in 1966, the district attorney subpoenaed three oral history interviews with Bowers from the Mississippi Department of Archives and History. Bowers had specified that the interviews be sealed until after his death. Attorneys for the archives argued that the subpoenas breached the agreement with Bowers and that in the future others would refuse to be interviewed if restrictions on access could not be guaranteed. Their motion was denied, and the interviews were turned over to the district attorney. Although they were not used at trial because Bowers did not take the stand in his own defense, the case shows that the courts will not respect agreements to seal interviews when they believe they contain evidence needed at trial.

The federal government and most states have laws granting access to government records. Under the federal Freedom of Information Act and state open records laws, any citizen can ask to inspect documents (with a few exceptions, such as personnel records) and bring a court action if access is refused. This makes it practically impossible for oral history programs operated by federal or state agencies to offer to seal or restrict access to interviews.[18]

In many states, but not at the federal level, journalists have enjoyed limited protection under shield laws that grant them the right not to reveal their sources in a legal proceeding. The laws recognize that it would be impossible for journalists to do their job—especially in covering topics such as crime and corruption—if their anonymous sources knew that a court could order their identity to be revealed. However, in some recent cases, shield law protections have been narrowed, with the courts holding that the need for evidence outweighs private arrangements between journalists and their sources. Even in states with shield laws, it is unclear whether the courts will extend the same protection for sources to oral historians.

What do you do if you are served with a subpoena for interviews that have been sealed or for which the interviewee was granted anonymity? If the court will not grant shield law protection or (as in the Bowers case) uphold the legal agreement between the interviewee and oral history program, the best course is to try to limit the scope of discovery. Neuenschwander recommends that in criminal proceedings, your counsel request *in camera* inspection (by the judge, not in the presence of the jury). In a civil case in which the program is not a party to the action, your attorney may be able to have the subpoena quashed by showing that the information can be obtained from other sources or that it is not material to the case; if the court rejects the motion to quash because it considers the information relevant, your attorney may request an in camera inspection. Neuenschwander concludes that oral history programs have limited ability to prevent court access to sealed interviews. He advises programs that regularly seal interviews to share with the interviewee "the remote but still very real prospect that a seal or access restriction might not prevent court access."[19]

INSTITUTIONAL REVIEW BOARDS (IRBs)

For years, oral historians working at colleges and universities in the United States have struggled with the IRBs that are responsible for regulating human subjects research. Regulations (the so-called Common Rule) are listed in chapter 45, section 46, of the Code of Federal Regulations (45 CFR 46). Eighteen federal agencies (though not the National Endowment for the Humanities) require institutions that receive federal funding for human subjects research to create IRBs to carry out the mandates of 45 CFR 46. In practice, most institutions have told their IRBs to apply the rules to all human subjects research, whether or not it is federally funded.

IRB members, usually with backgrounds in the medical and behavioral sciences, have tended to apply the rules of their own disciplines to the very different field of oral history. IRBs, according to oral historians Donald Ritchie and Linda Shopes, "have required oral historians to submit questions in advance, not to ask questions about sensitive or difficult topics, not to use interviewees' real names (despite their willingness—even eagerness—to be identified), and not to save the tapes once the project is completed."

All this, of course, is completely antithetical to the practice and standards of oral history—indeed, of history in general. Oral historians have had to file paperwork and appeals to seek exemptions from review, a process that has often delayed research. Rulings, write Ritchie and Shopes, "have been inconsistent from university to university, and sometimes from board to board within the same institution."[20] IRBs, they further attest, have had a "chilling effect" on research, with some historians deciding not to conduct interviews to avoid the bureaucratic hassles.

Mounting complaints led to a 2003 meeting between representatives of the Oral History Association and American Historical Association and the U.S. Office for Human Research Protection (OHRP), part of the Department of Health and Human Services (HHS). The OHRP ruled that oral history projects in general do not involve the type of research defined by the HHS regulations and are therefore excluded from IRB oversight.[21]

The regulations define research as "a systematic investigation, including research development, testing and evaluation, designed to develop or contribute to generalizable knowledge." This type of research typically involves standardized questionnaires with close-ended questions, a large sample of individuals who often remain anonymous, and a quantitative analysis. Oral history research, by contrast, is less systematic and structured, with open-ended questions and interviewees who agree to be interviewed (or, in the language of IRBs, give "informed consent") because of their knowledge of a topic or life experiences. Although all interviews may have some common questions, other questions are unique to each interview. It is impossible to know in advance how an interview will develop, so each interview provides a unique perspective. Unlike scientific research, the results of oral history interviews can rarely, if ever, be tested, evaluated, or become "generalizable knowledge."

Despite the OHRP ruling, many IRBs continue to review oral history research proposals for compliance with the rules for human subjects research. Certainly, projects in which oral history is one of several research methods used are subject to IRB review. They may be ruled exempt, but that determination must be made by the IRB. Indeed, at many institutions,

IRBs use a broader and more cautious definition of research than the "generalizable knowledge" standard of OHRP and insist on vetting oral history proposals.

Oral historians working at universities and colleges should plan to obtain informed consent forms from their interviewees in addition to the legal release. Although it can be argued that a verbal agreement (usually in a preinterview phone call) is informed consent, you will be doubly safe if you use a short form that explains the purposes of the project and asks the interviewee to agree to be interviewed. This is *not* a substitute for the release form. All it does is document the interviewee's agreement to be interviewed, and it says nothing about who will own the interview or how it will be used. Legally, the interviewee should sign the informed consent form before the interview begins.

Informed Consent Form

The ______________ oral history project is sponsored by [organization name]. Its purpose is to collect interviews with people who have knowledge and experience of [topic]. The recordings will be used for scholarly and educational purposes as determined by the project.

Your signature indicates that the purposes of the project and the use of the recordings have been explained to you and that you have agreed to be interviewed. You may discontinue participation in the interview at any time without penalty.

______________________________ ________________

Signature Date

______________________________ ________________

Signature of parent or legal guardian Date

NOTES

1. Bruce Sanford, *Libel and Privacy* (New York: Law and Business, 1991) (and supplements), 4.13.

2. John A. Neuenschwander, *Oral History and the Law,* 3rd ed. (Carlisle, PA: Oral History Association, 2002).

3. Ibid., 19.

4. Sanford, *Libel and Privacy* (1999 supplement), 4.12.

5. Neuenschwander, in *Oral History and the Law,* includes a discussion of invasion of privacy (23–25). Because oral history interviews are conducted with the interviewee's consent (and often in the interviewee's home or workplace), privacy issues are unlikely to arise. However, Neuenschwander identifies two areas of privacy law—disclosure of intimate private facts and false light—that potentially apply to oral history interviews and reviews the relevant cases.

6. See Neuenschwander, *Oral History and the Law,* 6–7, for an analysis of the four elements—agreement, consideration, competent parties, and lawful objective—that are necessary to make a legal release enforceable as a contract.

7. The Copyright Act of 1976 (as amended) is codified at Title 17 of the U.S. Code. The major exception to the Copyright Act is the federal government: all works prepared by government employees as part of their duties are considered part of the public domain. However, there are several exceptions, including a National Archives procedure allowing oral historians working for the federal government to offer interviewees copyright protection and the right to impose restrictions on access. See Neuenschwander, *Oral History and the Law,* 35–36. State and local governments have copyright protection for interviews by their employees.

8. 17 U.S.C. 101, 102; U.S. Copyright Office, *Compendium of Copyright Office Practices* [Compendium II] (Washington, DC: U.S. Copyright Office, 1984), § 317.

9. Neuenschwander, *Oral History and the Law,* 11.

10. 17 U.S.C. 105, 106.

11. See Creative Commons, "About Licenses," *Creative Commons,* http://creativecommons.org/about/licenses/.

12. 17 U.S.C. 107.

13. Neuenschwander, *Oral History and the Law,* 11.

14. U.S. Copyright Office, "Publications from the U.S. Copyright Office," *Copyright,* http://www.copyright.gov/pubs/html.

15. Peter Hirtle, "Copyright Term and the Public Domain in the United States," *Cornell Copyright Information Center,* http://www.copyright.cornell.edu/public_domain/.

16. Creative Commons, "Copyright-Only Dedication," *Creative Commons,* http://creativecommons.org/licenses/publicdomain.

17. Neuenschwander, *Oral History and the Law,* 14–15.

18. Two states, Kentucky and Texas, have enacted laws to protect sealed or restricted interviews from freedom-of-information searches.

19. Neuenschwander, *Oral History and the Law,* 14–16.

20. Oral History Association, "Questions Regarding the Policy Statement," http://alpha.dickinson.edu/oha/org_irbquestion.html.

21. Jeffrey Brainard, "Federal Agency Says Oral-History Research Is Not Covered by Human-Subject Rules," *Chronicle of Higher Education,* October 31, 2003.

Chapter Five

Interviewing

By David H. Mould

In Robert Redford's Oscar-winning 1988 film, *The Milagro Beanfield War* (based on the novel by John Nichols), graduate student Herbie Platt arrives in a dusty, dirt-poor New Mexico hamlet. With his tape recorder slung over his shoulder, he is ready to start research. But no one told the people of Milagro (population 426) he was coming, and no one seems to care. "I'm from NYU's Department of Sociology," he tells the mayor. "I'm writing a thesis. I'm supposed to be here for six months. I've got a grant." The mayor isn't impressed and offers no help.

Herbie doesn't know it, but he is walking into the middle of a classic late-twentieth-century western showdown between local residents and big business over water rights and real estate development. Despite being an outsider, he eventually earns the trust of the people of Milagro. It's not the title of his thesis, "Indigenous Cultures of the Southwest," that wins them over, but his willingness to accept their culture and living conditions.[1]

Most oral historians experience Herbie's predicament, though usually in a milder form. Interviewing, to put it bluntly, is a deliberate act of involvement in other people's lives. But interest in so-called traditional ways of life by well-meaning outsiders can be an imposition. The Inuits of Nunavut (Canada's eastern Arctic) have an old joke: The typical Inuit family consists of a father, mother, two children, and an anthropologist.

Unless you are a member of a community—a physical community such as a neighborhood or a community of interest such as a church, labor union, or quilt guild—you are an outsider without a clear connection to the people you want to interview. Why would people who don't know you take the time to talk to you? And what right do you have to ask about memories that may be uncomfortable or traumatic to recall? To understand why people are willing to talk, we need to understand that the interview is not a one-way process. It is an exchange or transaction.

THE INTERVIEW AS TRANSACTION

After his brush-off by the mayor, Herbie remembers the textbook advice from Anthropology 101: A researcher needs to build relationships before asking people questions. He spends several weeks working in the beanfield and getting to know the people of Milagro before pulling out his recorder to interview the oldest local resident, Amarante Córdova. It's a practical choice because Amarante evidently has time on his hands and even spends part of the day talking to the ghost of a departed friend.

He tells Herbie how the people of Milagro developed a homegrown variety of Catholicism in which the saints welcome offerings of tamales, salsa, and beer. In return, Herbie offers companionship to an old man who lives alone and finds that young people are too busy to talk. "You actually talk to the angels?" asks Herbie. "Those are the only ones around who've got time to talk," Amarante says.

In some communities, older people are interested in talking and have the time to do so. But companionship—the pleasure of spending an hour or two with an interviewer—is not the only benefit. Herbie is interested in how local religious traditions blend Catholic and animist rituals. Amarante feels he is passing on cultural knowledge that his young interviewer will respect and preserve. For older people, the interview is often a validation of their lives—the opportunity to pass on what they have learned and experienced to future generations. In a world where technology and communication continue to transform the way we live, work, play, and relate to each other, it is important to document how our grandparents and their grandparents viewed their worlds. This should not be an exercise in idealizing the past, adorned with clichés such as "It was a hard life, but it was a good life" or "Families were really families then." There's a lot about the past that is decidedly not pleasant—grinding rural poverty, domestic abuse, dangerous work in mines and factories, high infant mortality, disease, and natural disasters. As oral historians, we need to document both the good and bad of the past.

There are other reasons why people will talk to you. One is money. In a frantic, multichannel media environment in which celebrities and sports stars sell their stories of infidelity, drug and alcohol abuse, miracle diets, and spiritual awakening to the highest bidder (often to help pay their legal bills), some people expect to be paid for interviews. As a general rule, avoid people who declare interview income on their tax returns. It's certainly OK to pay for a meal or offer gas money if the interviewee had to travel to meet you. But a cash payment (or honorarium, to use a more polite term) not only depletes your project funds but also changes the relationship. The interviewee is now providing a professional service and is more likely to tell you what she or he thinks you want to hear, not what they believe or experienced. Paying for an interview also creates what I call oral history market distortion. If you pay one person, shouldn't everyone else you interview also expect payment? And how much? Will you pay by the hour? An unscrupulous interviewee will soon figure out how to stretch a one-hour interview into a three-hour marathon. It's best not to offer payment in the first place.

I'll offer two exceptions to this rule. An interviewee may have to give up income—even a day's work—to talk with you. If that's the case, then payment is justified, though a gift card may be a better choice than cash. In *Milagro,* Herbie paid for access through his labor in the beanfield. In other cultures, you need to offer cash or gifts. In West Africa, the griots are the guardians of clan and community history and expect payment for their stories. The much-interviewed Inuit also expect compensation. It doesn't seem an unreasonable request: The Inuit have seen many researchers come and go without sharing their work or putting anything back into the community.

People will also talk because they want to push a political or social agenda and see your project as a way to reach a broader audience. It may be a controversial local issue such as urban redevelopment, residential segregation, school funding, or whether to open a casino next to the senior center. Or it may be a national issue—foreign policy, taxes, free trade, school prayer, health care, or social policy—and the interviewee hopes that your project will add to other voices pressuring the Congress, the White House, and the Supreme Court. Either way, the interviewee is not a neutral observer but has an agenda. You do not have to agree or disagree with it; indeed, you should avoid expressing your own opinion in the interview. But recognize that this is the transaction. You get your interview. The interviewee gets to grind an ax.

There are similarities in how oral historians and psychiatrists conduct interviews, even if their goals are different. As James Lomax and Charles Morrissey point out, both prefer neutral and open-ended questions that do not direct or lead. For example, "Tell me about your father" allows the interviewee to answer freely, while "Did you have a good relationship with your father?" invites a socially appropriate answer.[2] This is not the place to delve into the extensive literature from several disciplines about how the interview can relieve stress, surface hidden emotions, and help people come to terms with troubling past experiences. Suffice it to say, there is compelling evidence that people who have been through life-threatening experiences such as wars and natural disasters often find relief in telling and sharing their stories. After extensive flooding in central West Virginia in November 1985, folklorist Michael Kline set out to interview the victims. Tucker County deputy sheriff Hank Thompson was one of eight people stranded in a house by the rising waters; through the night, the group huddled and prayed in an upstairs room as floodwaters shook the foundations, and trees and buildings crashed into the walls. They believed they would all die. After his rescue, Hank wondered why no one asked about his experience: "[N]ot one time has anybody come up to me or any of these seven other gentlemen that was in the house and said, 'Hey, you want to talk about it?' Not one time. And I know that there's people out there that also had a worse night probably than I did. And I would love to know who they are so that I could go talk to them. Everybody that was a victim or involved in this flood, in my opinion, should sit down and talk about it."[3]

YOU DON'T DIG UP INTERVIEWS

Much of the evidence historians use has been deliberately preserved. In this category are national, state, and local government documents; business and legal records; the files of religious, charitable, and labor organizations; books; art; movies; newspapers; magazines; television and radio programs; and physical objects. Some agencies and organizations are required by law to keep records. Other documents and objects are collected by museums, libraries, and archives.

A second category of evidence is literally discovered—carefully excavated in an archaeological dig or accidentally unearthed by a farmer plowing a field, washed ashore with the driftwood, or found in an attic, basement, or building being demolished. This kind of evidence—diaries, family photos, antiques, old tools, commercial signs, and catalogs—was not deliberately stored for future use because no one thought such commonplace items were worth sending to a museum. However, it becomes historically significant (and perhaps valuable) upon discovery.

The interview is another kind of historical evidence. Unless you stumble across a stack of forgotten reel-to-reel tapes with interviews with World War I veterans or find out that the audiocassette labeled Hot Country Rock actually contains an interview with your grandmother, there are no interviews to be discovered or dug up. There are only interviews that have already been recorded and those that will be recorded. And each is a unique historical document unlike any other interview.

The *unique* nature of the interview is worth stressing. No interview can be exactly the same as another interview. Even if the same two people—interviewer and interviewee—are involved, and the topics are the same, there will be differences—if not in substance, at least in nuance. A change in location or time may also change the way the interview goes.

There are many variables that make each interview unlike any other previously recorded and unlike any that will be recorded in the future. The age, gender, race, and social class of both interviewer and interviewee shape the interview, although not always in the way we expect. Because I'm a man, I'm aware that there are topics some women would rather discuss with a woman interviewer than with me. On the other hand, they may talk about issues they would not mention to a woman interviewer because they seem too obvious; because I'm a man, they feel the need to explain them to me. As a Caucasian, I can't claim to understand how an African American, Asian American, or Hispanic American experiences the world. But that does not mean I cannot interview members of other racial or ethnic groups. The proposition that only African Americans should interview African Americans or only gays should interview gays is a restrictive—indeed, elitist—notion. Taken to its logical conclusion, the "you need to be one of them to understand them" argument would mandate that only children should interview children and only current or former coal miners should interview coal miners. My interview with someone who is different from me—by gender, race, ethnicity, nationality, occupation, or any other measure—is no more or less valid than one conducted by an interviewer whose profile matches that of the interviewee. It is simply different.[4]

Sometimes unfamiliarity can be an advantage—the so-called stranger value. Anyone who has ever tried interviewing a close friend or family member soon realizes that the formal nature of the interview can produce tensions. "That's because," writes Jackson, "the role of interviewer puts you outside the role of a friend and makes for a situation more unnatural than that between a near-stranger and a person willing to talk about something that matters."[5] Friends and relatives are more likely to tell you what they think you want to hear or to be reluctant to criticize another family member or friend. It is difficult to separate the person they know from the interviewer. "Why are you asking me all these questions when you already know what happened?" is a typical reaction. With a stranger, none of those assumptions or relationships exists. Interviewing colleagues, coworkers, or members of your religious or social group poses similar problems because you share a body of knowledge or beliefs. Morrissey recalls an oral history project in which colleagues interviewed each other: "[T]he results were some rotten interviews. Some questions and answers were so obvious to both of them, neither the question was posed nor the answer given. The future historian is left perplexed." Morrissey is a firm advocate of a "clinical relationship" between interviewer and interviewee.[6]

The interview is inevitably a joint creation between interviewer and interviewee. Oral historian Michael Frisch uses the term *shared authority.*[7] That's a good way to describe a process in which the interviewer has a considerable role in shaping the interview—not only because of who she or he is but because of the topics selected, the questions asked, and the interviewing style. Except in rare cases, the interview is never simply a record of the interviewee telling a story. The interviewer shares authority in the interview. That's why in most oral history projects (see chapter 4), both interviewee and interviewer sign a release form transferring rights to the interview to the organization sponsoring the project.

What about interviewing more than one person—a couple, siblings, friends, or a group of people? There are some reasons for doing a group interview, but more for not doing it. In the planning stage of an oral history project, it can be helpful to bring together people with shared experiences—members of a trade union or religious group, or World War II veterans—to identify topics and themes for individual interviews. Sometimes these sessions are productive, as one person's memory triggers another's. But recording is challenging because of the number of speakers; unless you use video, it is difficult during transcription to be sure who's talking. Of course, in any group, some people speak more or more loudly than others, while some defer to others. A "hierarchy of status may emerge," according to Morrissey, "with the person with senior status (due to age, wealth, authority, or accomplishments) dominating the discussion and others reluctant to diverge from the consensus being established."[8] Group interviews may provide useful information, but the complex interpersonal dynamics make analysis difficult. You end up wondering what one person might have said if another person had not been present. The "others in the room" problem is even greater when you interview people who are related or have other close ties. The presence of a husband, wife, parent, sibling, or friend influences what they say in ways that they may not even realize.

In some societies in the developing world, according to Hugo Slim and Paul Thompson, "individual interviews are considered dangerously intimate encounters," especially for women. Tradition demands that one or more observers be present, but this may lead to censorship. The oral historian needs to pay attention to a society's communication modes and practices. If stories are told only in a group setting or only when certain people are present, that tradition must be respected. There may also be rituals for turn-taking and the order of topics. Slim and Thompson note that communal histories gathered in this way can result in pressure for the group to agree on a particular version of the past or "a powerful process of myth construction which misrepresents the real complexity of the community."[9] Still, in some societies, the group interview may be the only option.

IT'S NOT A CONVERSATION, IT'S A NARRATIVE. AND THERE'S AN AUDIENCE

The best interviews are conversational in style, but they are never conversations. An interview is, by definition, a more formal event than a conversation; it has been arranged in advance, and both interviewer and interviewee know the general topic if not the specific questions. It's a good idea to have a conversation—about a safe topic such as weather, sports, or food (stay away from politics or religion)—to break the ice with an interviewee you're meeting for the first time while you're setting up your equipment. But once the recorder is switched on, both interviewer and interviewee make the transition from conversation to interview. Edward "Sandy" Ives describes how he moves into interview mode by picking up the microphone and recording the time, date, place, and the name of interviewee: "Then I put the mike back in its place, sit back and relax, and continue, 'O.K., now that's taken care of. Now . . . ' I try to do it all in an offhand, diffident way. At the same time, I have made it unmistakably clear that the interview has begun."[10]

Ives's routine, as Jackson puts it, "nicely separates the interview from the conversation preceding it." Interviewee and interviewer are shifting from the regular time of conversation to the "ritual time" of the interview. In ritual time, the interviewer can "ask far more questions about far more subjects and in far greater detail than would be permissible or reasonable in conversation. . . . [Interviewees] don't automatically think you're stupid if you ask for a step-by-step explanation of a process or if you ask the name of things . . . . Very often people will shift their eyes from you to the microphone when these questions are asked, as if to say, 'I know Edna here understands this, but this explanation is for you people out there in tape-land.'"[11]

This awareness of the audience—the people out there in tape-land—turns the interview into a *trialogue* with the audio or video recorder as a silent but active third party. Some interviewees are more conscious of this than others, but all are aware that what they say will be shared with other people who are not in the room. The audience may be small—a few researchers or local historians—or large if the interviews are used in a public exhibit, a television or radio program, or a Web site.

This sense of audience may lead the interviewee to perform and talk in a more colorful or expressive manner than in normal conversation. In some oral traditions—from the West African griot to the Jack Tales of Southern Appalachia—this performance element is highly valued. Indeed, *how* the story is told is often almost as important as the story itself. Bearers of folktales and oral traditions have a repertoire of stories they have told many times in many settings. They are accomplished performers and have practiced their art; each story has a well-refined structure, rhythm, and tone, and it is designed to make an audience laugh, cry, or think about an issue. Inevitably, such an interview will be a performance. There's nothing wrong with that as long as we're upfront with the audience and let them know that the interviewee is a professional.

However, the trialogue can work the other way around and make the interviewee more cautious and less willing to share with an audience. In the business world, information about patents, processes, and products is proprietary. Intellectual property may be sold or licensed, but it is rarely given freely to an interviewer unless the interviewer is the corporate historian. The reason is clear: This information has a marketplace value, and disclosing it could help the competition. In a different context, folklorist Dennis Tedlock recalls how a Zuni interviewee told one version of a story for a Zuni audience and a censored one for a recording session: "Andrew had been mindful of the larger audience that might lie somewhere on the other side of that tape-recorder, an audience that might include the kinds of Anglo-Americans he had met up with in the government boarding schools, back in the days when Indian students were treated to mandatory Sunday-school attendance, corporal punishment and even confinement in on-campus jail cells. . . . the presence of a tape-recorder and the eventual goal of publication raise larger questions of what might be called interethnic rapport."[12]

SETTING UP THE INTERVIEW

Before the interview can take place, there's preparatory work to do. Unless someone hands you a list of interviewees with interview times and places already arranged, you'll need to make the contacts yourself.

Let's assume you have the name and contact information of a person you want to interview. The best way to set up an interview is for another person who knows the interviewee to introduce you. But usually you need to make a cold call without an introduction. With professional people, sending an e-mail is a good way to introduce yourself and your project. However, e-mails can be ignored (or end up in the spam folder), so a phone call is usually a better approach.

On the phone, you face the classic telemarketer challenge: saying enough in the first fifteen to twenty seconds to make sure the listener does not hang up. Because you'll likely be calling at the same time as telemarketers (around dinner time), you need to make sure your pitch is distinctly different. So skip the clichéd, "How are you doing today?" and quickly introduce yourself, the project, and how you got the person's name.

In fifteen to twenty seconds, you can introduce yourself, briefly describe the project, and provide a personal reference. That is often crucial to setting up the interview. Someone who is reluctant to talk to a stranger may be more inclined to stay on the phone if he or she knows that a neighbor, friend, or community member provided his or her name. It's also clear that you're not selling anything except the project. Now you can talk more about the project and describe its goals and the intended audience. But keep it short; don't overwhelm the interviewee with details. Then ask for permission to record an interview.

Even interviewees who seem interested may be reluctant. A common reaction is, "Why do you want to talk to me? I'm no expert." The idea that history is made only by great (and usually white) men (politicians, generals, and intellectuals) and significant events is still alive and well in the culture. We are so used to seeing the parade of so-called experts—on politics, business, technology, gardening, food, and fashion—on TV that the perspectives of ordinary people don't seem to count for much. This is where you make the point that you are deliberately *not* seeking expert opinions but want to document the experiences of ordinary people which are, after all, more representative. For some projects, you can add that you're trying to fill a gap in the historical record by listening to the voices of people and groups that have long been ignored by historians. That's not what you'll say if you are interviewing political and business leaders, but it's the goal of many community history projects.

Once the interviewee has agreed to the interview, set a date and time and give your phone number in case she or he has to reschedule or has questions about the project. If you're going

Interviewing is tiring work, so generally an interview should last no more than sixty to ninety minutes. Unless, that is, you're interviewing someone like Johnie Miller, whose family has farmed mountain pastures near Seneca Rocks, West Virginia, for two generations. From the main road, it took interviewer Michael Kline almost an hour (in a four-wheel-drive vehicle) to make the three-and-a-half-mile journey up the mountain on a rough track washed out by summer rains. In remote areas, coming back for a second interview is usually not an option. *Courtesy of Talking across the Lines*

to the interviewee's home or place of work and don't know the area, make sure you have directions. Call ahead to confirm the arrangement. Although the interview may be the most important thing you're doing that day, the interviewee has other priorities—a medical or family emergency, a surprise job interview, or a field of corn to be harvested. If you have to reschedule, don't sound too disappointed. You've saved a trip and still have an interview appointment.

If the interview is confirmed, keep the date free from other distractions. There's nothing worse than having to cut short an interview that's going really well because you scheduled another interview or need to pick up the kids for their soccer game. You'll likely need to return for a follow-up interview and can't be sure that the interviewee will be in such fine form again. However, there's no problem in telling the interviewee in advance that you expect the interview to last sixty to ninety minutes because that's about as long as most interviews should go. Then leave yourself two hours.

Background research on the interviewee and the topic is an essential part of planning. There are the usual sources—newspapers, other historical records, and other interviews. This research not only helps you plan topics and questions but also shows the interviewee that you have a serious interest in the topic. If, for example, you're going to interview someone about a particular occupation, spend time learning about the occupation. It's a sign of respect—to the interviewee and what she or he knows.

What to Take to the Interview

- Equipment—audio recorder or camcorder, microphones, microphone stand, cables, connectors, headphones, extension cords, digital camera
- Supplies—tape or digital storage, batteries, notebook, pens
- Project brochures or description
- Release forms
- Business cards
- Change for parking and photocopying

Leave enough time to assemble and test your equipment. It's worth taking a simple brochure or one-page description of the project so that the interviewee can pass it along (with your contact information) to other potential interviewees. If the project has a Web site, print out a couple of pages because you can't be sure your interviewee has computer skills or Internet access.

CONDUCTING THE INTERVIEW

The interview should begin with a short introduction. This is not just for your own record-keeping; it will determine how the interview is indexed in a database and serve as a guide for future researchers. You need a standard format so that the same information is recorded at the beginning of each interview. Other information that may be needed depends on the project.

How much structure is needed in an interview? Should you write down a list of questions? And do you need to stick to the list however the interview goes? These are common dilemmas

Introducing the Interview

- Name of interviewer
- Name of interviewee
- Brief biographical data, such as age and occupation
- Location of interview (be as specific as possible)
- Date of interview
- Brief summary of topic(s)
- Title of oral history project

interviewers face, and there are no simple answers. Much depends on the topic. If you are researching a specific event or issue, you'll need to ask common questions in all interviews so that you can compare the experiences and perspectives of the interviewees and organize material according to themes. This does not mean that you can't ask other questions; you simply have to make sure that the basic questions are covered. However, if you're conducting a life story interview, it's difficult to structure because each interviewee's life is different; beyond the basic details of birth, marriage, family, and occupation, there aren't many common questions to ask. Jackson distinguishes between two types of interviews. The *directive interview* has specific questions, and "the interviewee's comments are welcome only insofar as they are answers to those specific questions." The *nondirective interview* is "totally open: the researcher listens, the subject talks."[13]

Written questions are helpful but should serve as a guide, not a script. You need to be ready to follow up, ask a probing question, or even repeat or rephrase a question if you don't feel the interviewee answered it adequately. I tend to write down topics or themes rather than specific questions and divide them into two categories—*must-ask questions* that will be posed to every interviewee, and *good-to-ask questions* I'll use depending on how the interview (and time) goes. You may need to rearrange the question order and drop questions if they've already been answered. Most interviewers quickly learn that their questions jog other memories so that the interviewee in answering question three also answers questions five and six and part of question eight while referring back to question one. You need to listen carefully and be flexible.

Most interviewees find it easier to talk about the concrete and the physical than the abstract. You can try asking about shifting cultural norms in the American family, economic globalization, and the information revolution, but such concepts are difficult to grasp. However, if you ask someone how their children behave compared to their own generation, why they shop (or don't shop) at Wal-Mart, and how often they use the Internet, you're asking concrete questions that address the broader issues.

Your first questions should be relatively simple; as you build rapport with the interviewee, you can move on to more difficult questions. By the same token, start with uncontroversial issues. You may want to learn more about the interviewee's murky past, but it will be a very short interview if your first question is about his conviction for fraud and racketeering. Build rapport, let the interviewee talk about his life, and half an hour into the interview, he may say, "Let me tell you about that [expletive] judge who sent me down." Now all you need to do is nod. Morrissey recommends that sensitive questions should not be grouped together but spread among easy questions. He uses a two-sentence format in which the first sentence explains why the question is being asked, and the second contains the actual question. On particularly sensitive topics, Morrissey presents the hypothesis that "a future historian" conducting research "would certainly want to hear you tell your side of the story in your own words so your viewpoint and role can be fairly assessed. Would you please tell this historian what history needs to know about this episode?"[14]

Open-ended questions give the interviewee freedom to reflect and explore a topic: for example, "How did people react when you talked about your wartime experiences?" They often prompt follow-up or *precision questions* that can clarify (who, what, when, where?) and confirm (how do you know?). *Close-ended questions*—for example, "Did you join the army?"—are used when essential information or clarification is needed. *Prompt* or *probe questions* encourage the interviewee to expand on an answer, give an example, or go into more detail. Verbs such as *describe, illustrate, discuss,* and *compare* are useful in framing probe questions. And questions are not the only way to jog

Interview Memory-Joggers

- Interviewee's family photographs
- Photographs collected from other interviewees
- Scrapbooks
- Old newspaper articles
- Old maps
- Tools and implements
- Historical timelines

the memory. Physical objects, photographs, or a tour of the attic or basement can spark memories and associations.

During the interview, give the interviewee 100 percent of your attention. If you fiddle with the controls on the recorder, shuffle papers, or look away, you're sending the nonverbal message that something else is more important than whatever the interviewee is saying. However, it's OK to jot down notes—a word or name to remember or to return to later in the interview. The attention should be as nonverbal as possible; try to avoid "ah-ha," "OK," "I see," and other verbal fillers that make transcription and editing difficult. Maintain eye contact, and look and act interested. But don't put up road signs, such as vigorous nods or shakes of the head, that indicate you agree or disagree with the interviewee's perspective.

Never switch off the recorder, unless the interviewee asks you to do so. Turning it off is another sign that what the interviewee is saying is not important. That's an editorial judgment that you cannot reasonably make while the interview is in progress. And you're not saving much—tape and digital memory are cheap.

Every profession and group has its own language or jargon—for example, to identify stages in an industrial process, classify a species, or name the spirits and deities. Computers, the Internet, and cell phones have introduced new terms and concepts. And then there's the acronym-laden language of government agencies. Ask the interviewee to explain or define terms you don't understand. Check the spelling of personal names. Do your best to identify precise locations. In a rural area, where a common direction may be to "turn right where the Jones place used to be before it burned down," the names of county and township roads and landmarks are important. Remember, too, that in an audio interview, the recorder is a blind third party,

What You Shouldn't Be Asking

1. *Questions that invite a yes/no response.* There are times when you need to ask such a question to decide where to go with the interview. For example, "Were you living on Maple Street when the floodwaters breached the levee?" You need to ask that to decide whether to go ahead with questions about the flood. But in most cases, a yes/no question is unrevealing. Try to rephrase the question so that the interviewee will offer a description rather than a monosyllabic reply.

2. *Multipart or compound questions.* Ask one question at a time. If you ask an interviewee in a single question where and when she was born, how many brothers and sisters she had, what their names were, what her father and mother did, and what it was like to live in a log cabin, you're going to cause confusion. An interviewee will usually answer either the last question in the series or the easiest or most interesting one.

3. *Questions you don't understand yourself.* This is where research is important. If you've done your homework, you'll know the basics of an industrial process or a group's religious traditions. If you don't understand something, don't ask complicated questions about it. You'll seem either foolish or pretentious.

4. *Really big, philosophical questions* (unless you're interviewing really big philosophers). Don't ask your interviewee for their worldview or their opinion on cultural hybridity. Again, you'll come off as rather pompous.

5. *Leading or loaded questions.* These questions contain a built-in assumption about the interviewee's experience or behavior and ask the interviewee to elaborate. "How much money have you stolen from the taxpayers?" is a leading question. But leading questions come in more innocent form. "How has coal mining influenced your life?" or "How hard was it to walk five miles each way to school, barefoot in the snow?" are also leading questions. Don't make assumptions.

On the other hand, it's OK to ask questions to which *you* already know the answer. Remember that you're asking questions on behalf of the audience. You may know about a topic from your research or other interviews, but the audience doesn't. Always ask yourself what questions your audience would want to ask. Then ask them.

and you must interpret the interviewee's visual gestures. If the interviewee says, "It was a huge fish—*this* long," you ask, "About two feet?" Or if the interviewee says, "He was about as far away as those trees, but I could see he was carrying a gun," you ask, "That'd be about one hundred yards, right?" However, interpreting gestures is a challenge when the interviewee describes a complex process, such as making furniture; in such cases, video or still photos are needed.

Perhaps the most common mistake is to talk too much and not listen enough. In Western culture, there's often an unconscious fear of silence. When someone finishes saying something, you follow up with a comment or question to avoid an awkward silence. In the interview, it's tempting to jump in with the next question as soon as the interviewee has finished speaking. What will happen if you wait a few seconds and give the interviewee time for reflection? It sends the signal that you're interested in learning more about what the interviewee has just said before moving on. It provides an opportunity to elaborate, give an example, or connect the topic to other experiences. It won't work all the time, but it's worth trying, especially when the topic has stirred emotion in the interviewee.

What should you do if the interviewee asks for your opinion on a topic or on an action or decision he or she has just described? Resist the temptation to start answering questions because this reverses the roles in the interview. And don't argue—even if you find an interviewee's views deeply offensive. If you argue, you'll lose rapport. Historically, it's more important to find out why the interviewee holds these views. "Ask for elaborations, clarifications, explanations," writes Morrissey. "Be a student in the presence of a teacher, not a lawyer cross-examining a witness for the opposition."[15]

What if the interviewee goes off on an apparent tangent about something that's not on your list of questions or perhaps not even related to the general subject area? Do you interrupt and redirect to the previous or the next question? Or do you grant the interviewee a few minutes of freedom and see where this leads? I recommend the latter course—within limits. What may seem a tangent may be the interviewee's way of leading into a story linked to the topic you're exploring; however, the interviewee needs to introduce new characters, events, and settings to get there. As Ives puts it, "You ask about one thing and you get another: why? If, for example, you try to hold to a neat chronological order and your [interviewee] keeps breaking out of it, rather than becoming exasperated at his disorderliness, try asking yourself what order *he* might be following. . . . [A]ssociations, avoidances, and substitutions can give you valuable information. Once again, it is a matter of letting go intelligently and (without insisting on an insight in every tangent) listening carefully."[16] But don't let the interviewee stay off the topic for too long. If after several minutes it's apparent that this really is a detour, then politely steer the interview back on track.

By listening closely, you will detect speech patterns and rhythms, the linguistic indicators that make each interviewee's voice distinctive. More important, you will begin to understand what an interviewee considers important. It may be different from what you expected. You may anticipate a long and detailed answer to one question but instead receive a brief one, spare on details. By contrast, the interviewee may give you a long and complex answer to what you thought was a short and simple question. The interview is a historical document with shared authority. The interviewee is not only responding to your questions but also telling you how he or she views the past and what's important in his or her life. The term *velocity of narration* is sometimes used to describe the ratio between the chronological or clock time of an event and the time devoted to it in the interview. An interviewee may telescope time by dismissing whole decades in a few sentences but then tell a ten-minute story about a brief but life-changing event. Similarly, as Jackson notes, the order in which facts are presented "is a fact itself, and often one of great importance; we understand different things from the order of facts if the order comes from the order of the interviewer's question sheet or if it comes from the informant's natural flow of associations."[17]

Most interviews end with questions that help reinforce the relationship between interviewer and interviewee. Ask if there's anything else the interviewee would like to say. Usually there isn't, but occasionally someone has been bursting to tell you a great story, and you simply haven't asked the right question. Ask if you can contact the interviewee again either to clarify details or for a second interview. Ask if there's anyone else the interviewee recommends for an interview. Ask the interviewee to sign the release form and if he or she wants to know anything more about the project. Thank the person for his or her time, and tell the person you've enjoyed meeting him or her. Even if the interview yielded little useful material, you have nothing to lose by being courteous.

Interviewing is tiring work for both interviewer and interviewee. That's why most interviews should last no more than sixty to ninety minutes. You can try taking a break and resuming for another hour or so, but focus and energy level may be lost. So unless you've driven hundreds of miles for the interview and won't be coming back again, don't plan for a marathon session.

NOTES

1. *The Milagro Beanfield War,* directed by Robert Redford (Universal City, CA: Universal Studios, 1988).

2. James W. Lomax and Charles T. Morrissey, "The Interview as Inquiry for Psychiatrists and Oral Historians: Convergence and Divergence in Skills and Goals," *Public Historian* 11, no. 1 (Winter 1989): 20.

3. Michael Kline, prod., *Hey, Do You Want to Talk about It? West Virginia Flood Narratives,* audio documentary (Elkins, WV: Talking across the Lines, 1986).

4. Many recent articles have explored the difficult issues of gender, race, and ethnicity in oral history interviewing. See, for example, Tracy E. K'Meyer and A. Glenn Crothers, "'If I See Some of This in Writing, I'm Going to Shoot You': Reluctant Narrators, Taboo Topics, and the Ethical Dilemmas of the Oral Historian," *Oral History Review* 34, no. 1 (Winter–Spring 2007): 71–93.

5. Bruce Jackson, *Fieldwork* (Urbana: University of Illinois Press), 68.

6. Tracy E. K'Meyer and Charles T. Morrissey, "An Interview with Charles T. Morrissey: Part II: Living Independently: The Oral History Career of Charles T. Morrissey," *Oral History Review* 26, no. 1 (Winter–Spring, 1999): 88; Charles T. Morrissey, "Oral History Interviews: From Inception to Closure," in *Handbook of Oral History,* ed. Thomas L. Charlton, Lois E. Myers, and Rebecca Sharpless (Walnut Creek, CA: AltaMira Press, 2006), 170.

7. Michael Frisch, *A Shared Authority: Essays on the Craft and Meaning of Oral and Public History* (Albany: State University of New York Press, 1990). The concept continues to be discussed and debated among oral historians. See, for example, Lorraine Sitzia, "A Shared Authority: An Impossible Goal," *Oral History Review* 30, no. 1 (Winter–Spring 2003): 87–101.

8. Morrissey, "Oral History Interviews," 174.

9. Hugo Slim and Paul Thompson, *Listening for a Change: Oral Testimony and Community Development* (Philadelphia: New Society Publishers, 1995), 62–66, 68.

10. Edward D. Ives, *The Tape-Recorded Interview: A Manual for Fieldworkers in Folklore and Oral History* (Knoxville: University of Tennessee Press, 1980): 50–51.

11. Jackson, *Fieldwork,* 89.

12. Dennis Tedlock, *The Spoken Word and the Work of Interpretation* (Philadelphia: University of Pennsylvania Press, 1983), 292.

13. Jackson, *Fieldwork,* 96.

14. Charles T. Morrissey, "The Two-Sentence Format as an Interviewing Technique in Oral History Fieldwork," *Oral History Review* 15, no. 1 (Spring 1987): 43–53; "Oral History Interviews," 178–81.

15. Morrissey, "Oral History Interviews," 177, 188–89.

16. Ives, *Tape-Recorded Interview,* 62.

17. Jackson, *Fieldwork,* 96.

ADDITIONAL RESOURCES

Atkinson, Robert. *The Life Story Interview.* Thousand Oaks, CA: Sage, 1998.

Dunaway, David K., and Willa Baum, eds. *Oral History: An Interdisciplinary Anthology.* Walnut Creek, CA: AltaMira Press, 1996.

Miller, Robert L. *Researching Life Stories and Family Histories.* Thousand Oaks, CA: Sage, 2000.

Ritchie, Donald A. "Conducting Interviews." In *Doing Oral History: A Practical Guide,* 85–108. Oxford: Oxford University Press, 2003.

Yow, Valerie Raleigh. *Recording Oral History: A Guide for the Humanities and Social Sciences.* Walnut Creek, CA: AltaMira Press, 2005.

Chapter Six

Transcribing Oral History

By Donna M. DeBlasio

TO TRANSCRIBE OR NOT TO TRANSCRIBE? THAT IS THE QUESTION

Transcribing an oral history can loom as a daunting task for anyone relatively new to collecting interviews. Anyone engaged in oral history needs to ask the question up front: to transcribe or not to transcribe? There are many reasons for not transcribing, including lack of time, lack of proper equipment, lack of money, or just plain disinterest. The decision to transcribe (or not) should be made fairly early, especially if the interviews are needed for a project, publication, or other public use. The goal of the program, budget, personnel, and needs should be the determining factors in the decision.

Generally, researchers prefer to use the transcript rather than the interview itself for many reasons. Researchers are often working under time constraints, and it is much easier and faster to go through a transcript than to listen for hours to the actual interview. While some prefer to do just that or are engaged in research or a project in which they need the interview itself, the transcript is far easier to use as a document. In the long run, despite the difficulties and issues surrounding transcribing, it is still the best way to reach the widest audience possible. Keep in mind that a transcript is easier to use than the original recording: The interviewee can correct and amplify what he or she said during the interview, and the project will have something to show for its efforts. In reality, if oral history does what it is supposed to do, the interviews should be transcribed.

There are instances in which a bare-bones transcript should be done. Preparing audio or video oral history interviews for the media is one such instance. In this case, the interviews are done specifically for the final product; the only parts that need to be transcribed are those that may appear in the production. Remember, if money is the issue, you should conduct only as many interviews as you can reasonably transcribe. This helps you avoid the tricky situation of having to decide which interviews are most important, and therefore worthy of transcription, while relegating others to second-class status. The fact remains, however, that choosing not to transcribe at all is a good way to ensure that relatively few people will use the oral history collection.

Prior to discussing the process of transcribing, there are several concepts that need to be defined and discussed. When oral interviews are transcribed, the finished product is usually referred to as a *verbatim transcript*. While the meaning of the term *verbatim* is clear, how it applies to a transcript is not. A verbatim transcript can run the gamut of including every single utterance, crutch word, false start, stammer, and other verbal cues to one that is so heavily edited there is little of the flavor of the original interview. Indeed, one school of thought says the transcript itself is a separate source, different from the original spoken word. There is truth in this statement. After all, one of the transcriber's jobs is to make the transcript readable, which, at the very least, means adding punctuation where necessary. To see the difference between the verbatim and transcribed

Why Transcribe?

1. Makes interviews more accessible to more people.
2. Makes interviews easier to use.
3. The interviewee can amplify or correct the original interview.
4. Despite changing technologies, a hard copy of the transcript will provide a permanent record of the interview.

examples, check out item number one of the style sheet at the end of this chapter.

Punctuation is necessary because it adds clarity to the transcript. Since most people do not verbally indicate punctuation, the transcriber has to use his or her judgment, based on knowledge of English grammar, about the type of punctuation mark and its correct placement. By doing this, the transcriber has already deviated from the original source, but there would be little point in doing the transcript without putting in punctuation. Indeed, some large oral history archives regard the transcript as the primary document, while others regard the recorded interview as the primary document.

The other issue with transcriptions is that it is often difficult to capture the flavor of the interview. After all, the written word cannot convey accent, tone of voice, inflection, and the like. For some projects, how something is said is at least as important as what is said. In cases like this, the interview itself is the research tool of choice. In fact, anyone utilizing oral histories is often free to consult the actual interview. For most projects and researchers, however, the transcript is still the most useful way to peruse oral history interviews. Generally, some end users prefer only the historical information in an interview and thus want the transcript, which is the easiest version of the interview to use. Others want a transcript that reveals the interviewee's personality. Somewhere in these demands is common ground for most researchers and other users.

There are essentially two extremes in the transcription universe. There are the transcripts so polished and heavily edited that they are easily readable but lack character and liveliness. Then there are transcripts that try to preserve as much of the original interview as possible, down to gurgles, burps, coughs, and other assorted vocal expressions. The transcriber has retained the essence of the original, but it may be difficult to read. The ideal transcript, then, reflects the tenor, flavor, and character of the interview yet is still readable. In producing a transcript, good transcribers will determine what is essential to keep and what may possibly be eliminated.

In deciding whether to produce a transcript, there is also the issue of cost. Transcribing is not inexpensive. At best it takes eight to ten hours to transcribe one hour of taped interview. A new dictation machine can run around $350. There are companies that specialize in transcribing oral history interviews, but using one of them can be more costly than doing it in-house, depending on the number of interviews to be transcribed.

Transcribing interviews that are in a digital format does bring down the cost of equipment needed. Some digital recorders come with software like Windows Media Player that allows you to download the interviews to a computer. The interviews themselves can be saved on a CD or USB flash drive so you can have a back-up copy of the interview itself.

YOU'VE DECIDED TO TRANSCRIBE. NOW WHAT?

Transcribing begins with equipment. (At this point we're referring to analog tapes and equipment, which are further discussed in chapter 7). You can actually transcribe using a tape recorder—*if* you want to damage the machine! All kidding aside, it is difficult to use a regular tape recorder for transcribing. If the transcriber will be typing the interview, using a standard tape recorder means having to manually operate the machine. There are foot pedals available for standard tape recorders, but these machines were never meant for the constant rewinding necessary for transcription. Make an investment in a transcribing machine, but be aware that not all transcribing equipment is created equal. First, if you are using standard-size cassette tapes, there are not a lot of equipment choices available. Most of the dictating equipment uses microcassette tapes, which you don't want. A new Sony standard cassette transcribing machine, with few bells and whistles, costs around $350. The machine comes with a foot control and head set. Note

What Makes a Good Transcriber?

1. Good typing skills, with emphasis on accuracy rather than speed
2. Knowledge of grammar, including spelling and punctuation
3. Ability to accurately hear recorded sound
4. Good word processing skills
5. Ability to hear qualities of the written word

that if you are also doing video interviews, it would be wise to have the interview dubbed to an audio format for transcribing.

If you are using digital equipment to record the interviews, you will need several things in order to do transcription. You will need a laptop or desktop computer equipped with a soundcard, software, and a microphone. Free transcription software is available on the Internet. See Express Scribe at http://nch.com.au/scribe/index.html and Transcriber at http://trans.sourceforge.net/en/presentation.php. With either of these programs, you can use a foot pedal or the keyboard itself for starting, stopping, and playing back the audio. However, you will still need headphones.

You've bought the equipment. Now you need a transcriber. The transcriber most likely will not be the interviewer, so keep the following considerations in mind. A good transcriber has good typing skills; accuracy is more important than speed. Knowledge of the English language—including spelling and proper use of punctuation—and the ability to hear sound clearly are very important. Other skills should include a broad general knowledge base, since the more one knows about a topic, the easier it is to transcribe. Familiarity with computers and the word processing program your project members are using is useful. Finally—and this where we enter the realm of the intuitive—a good transcriber has an ability to retain the distinctive qualities of the spoken word and can convey them in written form.

As transcribing proceeds, keep several things in mind. Transcribing is more of an art than a science; in some ways it is comparable to translating from one language into another. The transcriber uses only words and punctuation to convey on paper what is essentially a spoken performance. Ideally, a transcript will reflect the speaker's character and preserve as much of the quality of the interview as possible yet still be readable. Above all, anyone doing transcription must never replace the interviewee's choice of words with one the transcriber happens to feel is a better choice. The main task is to produce a verbatim transcript—it is essential to type the words in the order in which they are spoken so that the meaning is not changed.

LET'S TRANSCRIBE (AKA TRANSCRIBING IS FUN-DAMENTAL!)

You have the equipment, and you have the interviews; now it is time to transcribe. Determine the form for the transcripts from the outset so that all of the transcripts look alike.[1] The header should include the following information: organization name, title of project, interviewee name, interviewer name, date of interview, topic within project (for example, if the project is on the Vietnam War, the topic might be Nurses in the Vietnam War), and catalog number (if necessary). Also determine how each speaker will be identified. One way is to simply use Q and A. Of course, this could get confusing since the interviewer does not always ask a question and there may be other conversation on the tape. A better way is to use the first initial of each speaker's the last name. If both speakers have the same initial, then also use the first initial of the first name. Double-space or triple-space the first draft of the transcript to allow the interviewee to make additions, corrections, etc. Set the left margin at 1 ½ inches; set the right, top, and bottom at 1 inch.

When transcribing, the number one rule is be accurate. Spell all words correctly. Punctuation should be consistent. As you transcribe, listen to a few minutes of tape to get a feel for the speaker's speech patterns, pace, inflections, and language. Type the words you hear in the exact order they are spoken. Absolutely do not replace the interviewee's words—for example, profanity, slang terms, and localisms—with synonyms. This kind of language helps to retain the flavor of the interview. Also, resist the urge to fix the interviewee's grammar. People often make grammatical errors when speaking that they would not make in writing. The rule of thumb is, if the grammatical error does not impede the ease of reading the transcript, leave it in.

For example, "I seen him"—meaning, "I saw him"—is a common spoken error. Leave it alone. On the other hand, do not indicate an accent or dialect by spelling it phonetically. For example, mispronunciations such as "I dunno" for "I don't know" should not be typed. Such misspeaking is exactly that, and the transcriber should type it in correct English.

To make the final document more readable, eliminate stammering, supportive words such as "humm," "uh-huh," and "errr." You can include crutch words such as "like" and "you know," but keep them to a minimum. Listen for the end of the sentence. Many interviewees go on and on using "and" or another conjunction to indicate a new thought. End run-on sentences with periods at reasonable intervals. Create a new paragraph when the subject changes. Type contractions as they are spoken (i.e., "isn't" instead of "is not"). Do not transcribe false starts or unfinished sentences if the interviewee clearly reconsiders, stops, and then restates information. Do transcribe information the person does not repeat in the revised sentence.

What happens if you can't hear something that was said? First, listen again. If you still can't understand, ask someone else to listen. Don't spend hours, however, trying to figure it out. Leave a blank space as long as you think is needed; perhaps the interviewee, interviewer, or editor will be able to figure it out. If none of this works and the tape is still inaudible, you can indicate the missing portions with: [inaudible]. For the correct spelling of proper nouns, consult the notes that came with the interview. If you don't have them in the notes, the interviewee may be able to fill them in.

The tricky part of transcribing is trying to convey the flavor of the interview. Convey unspoken messages through punctuation such as ellipses, dashes, and the like. Indicate inflection and tone of voice by the exclamation mark, if appropriate.

Transcribe audible expressions and actions by typing notes to the reader in as few words as possible and placing them in parentheses—for example: (laughter). At the end of the interview, type and center the words "END OF INTERVIEW" in capital letters on the last line.

IT'S A MATTER OF STYLE

One of the major decisions any program needs to make from the outset is to determine the style to be used for transcripts. I suggest picking a style guide from the outset and sticking with it: Consistency is a virtue. There are a number of style guides available. Historians and their students normally use the most recent edition of *The Chicago Manual of Style*. Kate Turabian's *A Manual for Writers of Term Papers, Theses, and Dissertations: Chicago Style for Students and Researchers* is a condensed version of the *Chicago Manual*. Those in the field of English rely on *The MLA Style Manual and Guide to Scholarly Publishing*. Journalists use *The Associated Press Stylebook and Briefing on Media Law*. Social scientists (with the exception of historians) use the *Publication Manual of the American Psychological Association*. You need to determine which style works best for your project. Style guides will literally spell out exactly how to use punctuation, how to put numbers into type (Do you use the numerals? Do you spell out the words?), when to capitalize, and many other points of English grammar. The guides also go into great depth on the proper style for citations and bibliographies.

THE TRANSCRIPT IS DONE. NOW WHAT?

Once the first draft of the transcript (what—there is more than one draft???) is completed, someone (not necessarily the transcriber) needs to audit check the interview. The auditor may or may not be the person who edits the transcript. Auditing combines hearing with verifying the record. The auditor must listen carefully to the tapes and check them against the transcript to make sure that spelling is correct, the words are in the correct order, no words were added, and punctuation corresponds to the sense and sound of the narration. The auditor should also consider whether or not the transcriber has left out (or left in) too many meaningless gurgles, false starts, and the like.

At this point, the transcript can be sent to the interviewee for review. Not every project or program necessarily performs this task. The advantage of this is that the interviewee can correct the spelling of proper names and places as well as possibly fill in any inaudible portions of the interview. Sometimes interviewees add information to the transcript. If this occurs, the final typist can integrate the material into the transcript where the interviewee indicates that it belongs or include the information in a footnote or endnote and indicate that the interviewee added the material to the transcript. If the interviewee deletes anything from the transcript, the program should respect the person's wishes and delete that information from the transcript. It is not feasible or realistic to delete material from the tape itself. But the transcript is usually the resource made available to the general public. A note can be included with the tape that indicates the interviewee wished to delete a portion of the interview. The draft transcript should remain with the file copy of the final draft and the paperwork in order to retain a record of the interviewee's alterations.

Once the interviewee returns the transcript in the stamped, self-addressed envelope the project provided for his or her convenience, the editor should read through the transcript and make sure that it is ready to be typed in final format with correct spelling, punctuation, and adherence to the program's style sheet. An editor must be a tolerant critic and change only what cannot be understood on first reading. Again, the editor will make sure the transcript retains the flavor of the interview. At times, the transcriber may have used excessive punctuation like ellipses, dashes, or commas and too many crutch words like "you know." These hinder readability, although they may give a more accurate account of the interview itself. Ultimately, the editor is to make sure that the transcript is readable but that the interviewee's meaning is not changed in any way.

When editing is complete, the transcript can be prepared in its final format. Each transcript should have a title page (see the sample at the end of this chapter).

On the first page of the transcript, type the name of the sponsoring institution in upper case letters on the first line. If you have two institutions, double-space between each line and include the word "and." Allow four spaces between the name of the project and the interviewee, and double-space between each name, subject, and date. Leave four spaces before typing the text of the transcript. Place page numbers on the lower right-hand corner. If a speaker's dialog continues from one page to the next, it is not necessary to retype that speaker's initials. Single-space the body of the transcript, and double-space between each speaker and new paragraphs.

After the final version of the transcript is complete, you may choose to index it. With word processing programs like Microsoft Word and WordPerfect, indexing is much easier since the software includes a limited indexing capability. Indexing is really helpful for anyone trying to work from the transcripts, although it is not a requirement.

The transcript is now complete and ready to be made available in whatever format the creators choose. The final printed version should be on acid-free, archival quality paper that ensures there is a permanent record of the interview in hard copy. You may choose to send a copy of the final typed transcript to the interviewee as a thank you for sharing his or her time and memories with you. And remember: Transcribing is fun.

Transcribing Steps in a Nutshell

1. Transcribe the first draft.
2. Have another person audit check the completed first draft.
3. Send first draft to interviewee with a self-addressed stamped envelope.
4. Upon return of transcript, have editor check for accuracy.
5. Make corrections to first draft.
6. Print copies of final draft on acid-free, archival quality paper, and send one copy to the interviewee.
7. And remember: Transcribing is fun.

NOTES

1. There is a sample transcript at the end of this chapter.

[SAMPLE TITLE PAGE]
YOUNGSTOWN STATE UNIVERSITY
ORAL HISTORY PROGRAM

YSU History Project
Youngstown College Football

O.H. 1955
Marilyn Chuey
Interviewed By
Erin Pogany
on
April 4, 2000

[SAMPLE FIRST PAGE]
Youngstown State University
Oral History Program
Project: YSU History
OH #1955

Interviewee: Marilyn Chuey
Interviewer: Erin Pogany
Subject: Youngstown College Football
Date: April 4, 2000

P: This is an interview with Marilyn Chuey for the Youngstown State University Oral History project on Youngstown College Football at Mrs. Chuey's Poland, Ohio, residence on April 29, 2000. Now I thank you very much for being here this afternoon.

C: You're welcome.

P: When is your date of birth?

C: April 2, 1929.

P: And where were you born?

C: Cleveland, Ohio.

P: Cleveland, Ohio, and did you move here after you were born then or where?

C: A couple of years after I was born in Cleveland.

P: OK, do you have any siblings?

C: I have one, but she is deceased.

P: OK, is she older than you?

C: Older, six and a half years.

P: And you moved to Youngstown then?

C: Yes.

P: OK, and where did you live in Youngstown?

C: We lived on Florida Avenue on the south side.

P: What was it like growing up there?

C: Everybody was nice. Everybody went to Sheridan School, which at that time was a pretty school. And we enjoyed it.

P: And what was a typical day like growing up there, when you were younger?

C: Generally, going to school, coming homing and playing softball.

P: Oh, how nice! You played?

C: Yes, I did.

P: Was it a neighborhood team?

C: Actually, it was just youngsters from the school that would come to a nearby playground, and we did play.

P: Oh, how nice! You were athletically inclined from a young age.

C: I would say so [laughter].

P: And we can state here for the record, who was your father?

C: Oh, Howard Jones.

P: Howard Jones, who was?

C: The first president.

P: Of?

C: Youngstown College, at that time.

Chapter Seven

Catching Sound and Light

By Charles F. Ganzert

Several years ago, a university professor located a cache of reel-to-reel audiotapes about the early days of the petroleum industry at the Lima Public Library in western Ohio. Oil exploration had spread from Pennsylvania to Ohio in the 1880s, and the tapes included interviews with oil wildcatters, drillers, explosives experts, boiler stokers, and metalworkers who had worked in the region between 1886 and 1917. They told stories about drilling, constructing derricks, making and transporting nitroglycerine, and building the first large iron storage tanks.

These narratives, collected by a folklorist in the early 1960s, were recorded on an inexpensive home recorder on three- and five-inch reels at a slow tape speed (3¾ inches per second). In analog (reel-to-reel) audio recording, tape speed significantly influences recording quality. At 3¾ inches per second, the audio signal is crammed into a small area of magnetic tape that does not accurately represent the range of the human voice, especially higher frequencies. Take the same audio signal and spread it out over twice as much tape (a recording speed of 7½ inches per second), and the quality improves; move up to 15 inches per second, and you'll have excellent quality. In analog audio recording, the rule is the slower the speed, the poorer the fidelity. The folklorist had saved tape by recording at a slow speed but had sacrificed quality. It took many hours to improve the sound on these oil exploration tapes so the stories could be used in a radio documentary called *Voices from the Oil Patch*.

The recording gear and the storage media we use determine how we will be able to use recorded interviews in the future. This chapter outlines technological issues in audio and video recording, including the analog and digital recording processes, as well as the purchase of equipment.

WHY YOU NEED TO KNOW THE TECHNICAL STUFF

Recording media are undergoing evolutionary changes as new devices are introduced and old machines and formats are abandoned. It can be a challenge to find a machine that will still play old recordings, such as 78-RPM records, eight-track tapes, digital compact cassettes, 16-millimeter film, Sony Betamax videotapes—or those slow-speed tapes from Lima. Which of today's recording formats will be antiquated tomorrow? That is difficult to know. What seems clear, though, is that we need to make the best-quality interview recordings we can afford and store them in the most permanent, flexible format we can identify. We should also hold on to old equipment to convert interviews into newer formats.

While some people cherish their analog audio discs and tapes, the battle between analog and digital recording is substantially over, and digital has won. The recording fidelity, variety of recording options, ease of editing and mixing, flexibility of storage, and list of playback and presentation options have persuaded most professionals to migrate to digital.

How do you know which digital recorder to buy to record interviews? How accurately will it reproduce all the qualities of the human voice? Which features will you need? Which should you pay for? And which are simply nice bells and whistles? Will it be easy to transfer your interviews from the recorder to other media for transcription, editing, and long-term storage? Which kind of microphone should you use in different recording situations? Every oral historian needs to make these decisions, and it's best not to rely on advice from someone who has a product to sell or a commission to make. You need to know enough about technical considerations to make informed choices and ask the right questions. That means learning about sound and light, digital sample rates and bit depths, storage memory, microphone design and pickup patterns, video recording formats, and other technical areas. And it all starts with the nature of sound itself.

THE NATURE OF SOUND

Sound is the movement of air molecules. These molecules travel in waves similar to those on the ocean or on a lake. The peak, or top, of each wave represents an area of high concentration of air molecules, and the bottom, or trough, of the wave represents an area of low concentration. When we look at the ocean on some days, the waves roll in and break against the shore quickly and often, but on other days, they come in slowly. The same can be said for sound waves. We measure sound waves by how quickly the waves roll in and how often they alternate from peak to valley. One peak and one valley is called a cycle; when we describe sound, we use the term *cycles per second.*

Complex sound waves travel through the atmosphere all the time, but humans are able to hear sounds only within a certain range. Most of us can hear the movement of air molecules in a range from 20 to 20,000 cycles per second, although our ability to hear higher-pitched sounds declines with age. At the low end of the range are sounds such as thunder and the low strings of a bass; at the high end (above 15,000 cycles per second) are the triangle and the high, crisp sound of a cymbal, as well as harmonics of lower musical notes. Animals such as bats, dogs, and elephants can hear sounds outside the range of human hearing.

The number of times a sound wave cycles from peak to valley in one second is called *frequency;* people hear the frequency of a sound as *pitch*. We perceive sound waves between 20 and 250 cycles per second as *bass;* we perceive high-pitched sounds, or frequencies roughly between 5,000 and 20,000 cycles, as *treble*. Cycles per second are usually expressed in units called hertz (Hz), after the German physicist Heinrich Hertz. The large sample numbers are usually expressed in a metric shorthand, so 20,000 cycles per second or Hertz is usually written as 20 kHz (or kilohertz).

The human voice covers a fundamental frequency range from 110 to 330 Hz with women's voices at the higher end. However, there are harmonics—additional frequencies that add tonal color and character—between 82 and 1,047 Hz.

AUDIO RECORDING

In traditional analog recording, such as reel-to-reel or cassette tape, the machine stores a continuous stream of magnetic information, and the signal rises and falls in the same manner as the sound waves it is reproducing. It gets the name *analog* because the electronic and magnetic signals are a mimic; they respond in ways that are *analogous* to the original sound.

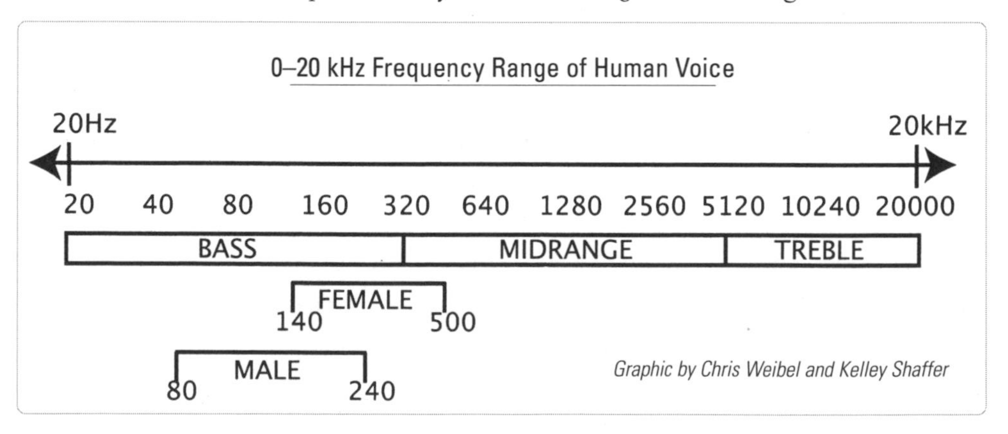

Graphic by Chris Weibel and Kelley Shaffer

Digital recording employs a different method of storage. Digital machines measure and store samples (or snapshots) of each sound. These samples are preserved and used later to create a reproduction of the original sound waves. The quality of a digital audio recording is determined by two things: the number of times per second that each sound is measured, or *sampled,* and the length of the description used to describe each sample, or *bit depth.* Commercial audio CDs are made up of files of data with 44,100 samples per second (44.1 kHz), and each sample is made up of 65,536 potential numerical values to describe what is happening to the sound wave during each sample.

The number of samples per second, or *sample rate,* determines the frequencies that a device can measure and record, particularly in the high range. To identify the number of cycles per second for a particular sound wave, a digital device must be able to identify its peak and valley. Each wave must be measured at least twice—during one peak and one valley—to do this. Therefore, the highest frequency that a device is able to register is determined by dividing the sample rate in half. Thus, CDs recorded at 44,100 samples per second (44.1 kHz) are able to recognize sound waves up to a frequency of 22,050 Hz. Since most humans can hear sounds in a range from 20 Hz to 20 kHz, a 44,100 Hz sample rate makes it possible to record sounds from the very lowest to the highest within the range of human hearing. Low frequencies are sampled more than the minimum, but the extra information adds clarity and definition to those sounds. High frequencies are measured at least adequately enough to identify each sound. This is how the CD sample rate was originally determined.

Each individual sample must be measured, and the values converted into data to be stored. The potential number of values a recording device is able to use to represent a sound affects the resolution of that recording. The number of binary bits used in the description of each sample is the *bit depth.* In measuring a sample, an 8-bit recording is able to record 256

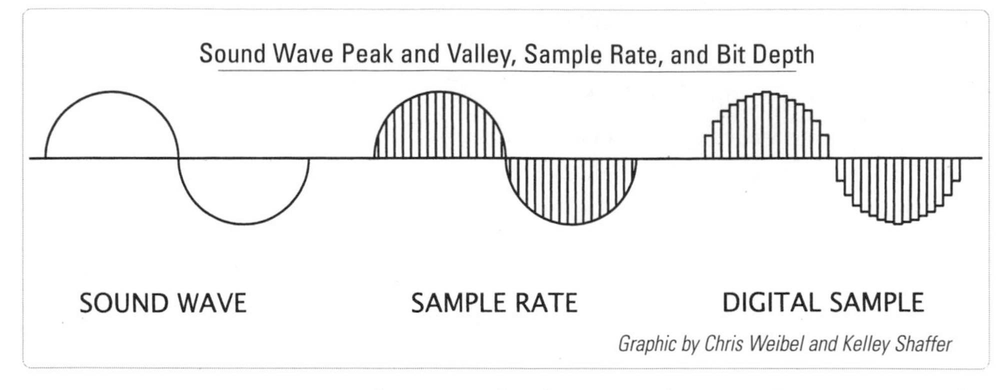

Graphic by Chris Weibel and Kelley Shaffer

potential numerical values, a 16-bit recording 65,536, and a 24-bit recording 16,777,216. The greater the bit depth, the better the recording quality. Bit depth also determines the maximum dynamic range (loud to soft) that can be recorded. A commercially produced music CD is in a 16-bit format.

If you think of digital recording as graphing the characteristics of a sound wave, the sample rate represents the vertical lines on the graph, while the bit depth represents the horizontal lines. The size of each square on the graph created by these horizontal and vertical lines influences the resolution of the recording.

Many digital recording devices allow the selection of a specific format and/or sample and bit depth. A file with a sampling rate of less than a 44.1 kHz and 16-bit rate (for instance, 32 kHz or 8-bit rate) is of lesser quality than the sound of a CD. Recordings with higher sample and bit rates (for instance, 48 kHz and 24-bit rate) reproduce additional frequencies more accurately.

CDs and DVDs are not the only digital storage formats available. The WAV (.wav) audio file format was created by the Microsoft Corporation for Windows, AIFF (.aif) files were developed by Apple, and MP3s were defined by the Motion Pictures Experts Group as a compression software for audio and film.

However, there is a trade-off in digital recording. High-quality recordings require more memory and fill up storage devices more quickly. Lower-quality recordings take up less space. For instance, a one-hour 44.1 kHz and 16-bit stereo recording takes up 605.6 megabytes of memory, while a one-hour 96 kHz and 24-bit stereo recording takes up 1.98 gigabytes. Audio files require significantly more computer memory than print documents but less than those for video.

The choice of sample and bit rates can depend on the sound source to be recorded. For instance, recordings on old 78- and 45-RPM records and cassette tapes are of comparatively low fidelity, so saving them in a high-resolution format beyond the CD standard may not enhance quality. On the other hand, new music and voice recordings will benefit from a high-resolution format and should be saved in that manner.

AUDIO EQUIPMENT

There are several factors to consider in selecting audio-recording equipment. What media will be used to share the recordings with others? What is the desirable level of quality? How much money is available? If all you need to do is to record and transcribe an interview, a small, inexpensive hand-held recorder like the ones used by newspaper reporters or students recording a class lecture will do the job. Most of these devices have built-in microphones, and a few enable you to select recording quality. Some MP3 music players and iPods can be converted into an audio recorder for a modest investment. However, the recording quality is relatively low.

If you purchase a machine capable of higher-quality recording, the interviews can be used in a variety of print and audio media, including radio, the Web, or CD. Several hand-held, professional field recorders meet radio news standards. These devices usually have built-in microphones, but some make it possible to plug in an external microphone. Though digital audio tapes (DAT) and MiniDiscs are currently available, many of the new professional field machines record directly to disc, hard drive, or flash memory cards. The memory cards are removable like the ones used in digital cameras or global positioning system (GPS) devices, and the interviews can be downloaded into a computer or other long-term storage device so the cards can be erased and reused. Similarly, files recorded directly onto a hard disc recorder will need to be transferred. When shopping for a machine, find out how easily files are transferred from the recorder into a computer for long-term storage.

A third approach is to purchase software that converts a laptop computer into a recording device. This requires a good-quality sound card and an external microphone that plugs into a microphone input on the side of a computer. Some podcast kits also allow you to connect a microphone to a universal serial bus (USB) port. With the right software package, you can record, edit, mix, and store audio files as well as burn them to a CD. One of the advantages is that you can select an external microphone appropriate for the recording situation. Another is that the software usually makes it possible to choose the file format in which the data is saved.

To use a computer as a recording device, you need an analog-to-digital (A/D) converter. This device also converts the stored digital information back into sound during playback. Proprietary software requires a sound card to do this job, but many inexpensive cards add noise and distortion to the signal. Professional quality systems use an external A/D converter to do the job.

The most powerful, flexible, and expensive systems combine hardware and software. The hardware includes an external, desktop device with good-quality microphone preamplifiers and A/D converters that plug into either a laptop or a desktop. These devices make it possible to bring a high-quality signal into the computer, but they also require an external microphone. Many manufacturers bundle their own software with the hardware, which assures maximum compatibility between all the component parts of the system. These studio-in-a-box work-

Digital Audio Equipment Options	
Small hand-held personal recorder	Easy to use, inexpensive, but poor audio quality; good for transcription only
Professional hand-held news recorder	Moderate expense, good audio quality, good for transcription and other types of digital distribution
Computer plus software combination	Laptop plus software can be expensive, some technical skill required; can be used to record, edit, and mix good audio quality
External hardware, software, and computer	Highest-quality recordings, bulky for field work but a powerful workstation that can be used for recording, editing, mixing, and transferring old recordings; technical skill required

stations allow you to convert a laptop computer into a powerful and flexible field recording machine that can do recording, editing, mixing, and signal processing at a price that would have been unimaginable a few years ago. Though more bulky than smaller handheld devices, they produce high-quality audio.

These systems usually accept both *microphone* and *line level* signals. A microphone level signal goes into a preamplifier before it reaches the computer. A line level signal is one that comes from a recorder, such as a cassette, reel-to-reel, MiniDisc, or DAT. These systems can import old archival analog recordings and convert them into digital ones as well as record live sound. In addition, all computer options allow you to burn the finished recordings to disc.

MICROPHONE CHARACTERISTICS

A recording chain is no stronger than its weakest link. The signal begins in the microphone, so the microphone helps determine audio quality. Microphones are classified by how they convert sound—the movement of air molecules—into an electrical signal. A *transducer* is a device that converts one form of energy into another, and that is what a microphone does: It changes sound energy into electrical energy. There are three types of professional microphones: dynamic, ribbon, and capacitor. *Dynamic* microphones use a moving coil of wire in a magnetic field. This principle, electromagnetic induction, is employed in the generation of hydroelectric power. But instead of a turbine revolving as a result of rushing water, a dynamic microphone includes a coil of wire attached to a diaphragm. The *diaphragm,* similar to an eardrum, moves in and out in response to sound waves; this physical movement of the coil causes electrons to flow.

A *ribbon* microphone also uses an electromagnetic transducer, but the coil of wire is replaced by a metal ribbon in a magnetic field. This ribbon acts as a diaphragm; when it moves, it causes electrons to flow. Ribbon microphones are good for vocal work but are fragile and not often used outside a studio setting.

The third type, a *capacitor* or *condenser,* works on an electrostatic principle that is less like a turbine and more like lightning. In the atmosphere, clouds filled with negatively charged particles ground themselves or release their charge during a storm, which we see as bolts of lightning. Similarly, a capacitor microphone is made up of two charged plates that cause electrons to transfer from one to the other as they move in and out. Sound waves striking one of the plates—which, again, is in the form of a diaphragm—cause this movement. The electrical signal created

Microphone Transducers

Dynamic	Moving coil in a magnetic field. Less expensive, rugged, good for fieldwork, slow response to transient/quick sounds.
Ribbon	Metal ribbon moving in a magnetic field. Good for voice work, less rugged, can be expensive, not suitable for fieldwork.
Capacitor or Condensor	Electrostatic transducer. Requires power, very sensitive, fragile, most expensive, less often used for fieldwork.

by this exchange, however, is weaker than that of a dynamic microphone, so a preamplifier boosts it to a workable level.

Generally, capacitor microphones are more sensitive than dynamic ones and so are able to pick up quieter sounds. However, they are typically expensive and fragile, and they are not often used in field recording. Dynamic microphones, on the other hand, are usually less sensitive to quiet sounds or noises that begin and end quickly, like a handclap or a gunshot. However, they are also less expensive, more rugged, and more often used in field recording.

Microphones also have directional characteristics. They can be omnidirectional, picking up sounds from all sides; bidirectional, sensitive from two sides; or unidirectional, picking up sounds from only one direction. *Omnidirectional* microphones are useful when the person being recorded tends to move around or in a situation in which you want to *include* background sounds. *Bidirectional* microphones are used for one-on-one interviews in which the individuals sit opposite one another. *Unidirectional* or *cardioid* microphones help *exclude* noisy background sounds during an interview. Many microphones attached to video cameras are inexpensive capacitor (or electret) unidirectional microphones.

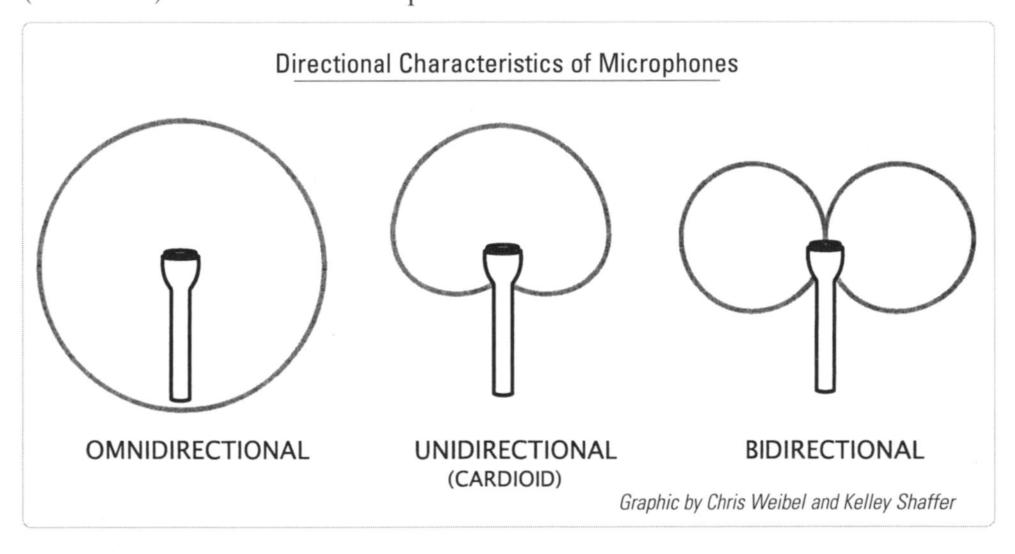

Graphic by Chris Weibel and Kelley Shaffer

The *lapel* or clip-on microphone is a small capacitor microphone designed to be attached to a shirt or jacket. It is often used for video recordings so that viewers do not notice the microphone. Lapel microphones are also used when interviewing people who are unaccustomed to media work. The microphone is small; it is easy to forget that it exists, so people tend to relax during the interview. However, inexpensive lapel microphones produce a signal of only moderate sound quality. Often, a good dynamic microphone offers better fidelity.

The decision to purchase a microphone for interview use, then, should be based on its intended use, likely recording situation, and budget.

THE VIDEO OPTION

When my wife's family decided to interview their Uncle Dan, one of the last remaining relatives of their older generation, they made a video of the interview, which they later copied and distributed to the whole clan. It is easy to see why a family speaking with a beloved relative would want to have moving images of that person to share. Though video gear is more expensive than audio, prices have gone down in recent years, while quality, ease of use, and functionality have improved.

Once again, although there are analog and digital systems on the market, it looks as if digital video has won the battle. The video process begins with shooting or acquiring images. Analog tape formats include VHS, S-VHS, Betacam SP, and Hi8. Examples of digital tape include Digital-8, and Mini-DV. Digital cameras are also available in direct-to-disc or direct-to-hard drive formats. One advantage of tape or disc master recordings is that they can be archived although they deteriorate over time. Direct-to-hard drive systems have distinct advantages when importing or *capturing* video clips into the computer, editing them, and converting them into a distribution or display format, but they are not used for long-term storage. However, once video has been captured, it does not matter what recording device the original footage came from.

If unedited interviews are the final product, archiving master tapes is a quick solution. However, if the video is to be edited or if the material needs to be converted into a different format for the Internet or burned to DVD, the most cost-effective solution is a computer with video editing and DVD authoring software. This video computer could potentially be the same one used for the audio work discussed earlier.

Both analog and digital video can be loaded into a computer, but digital is easier to manage. Using a FireWire or USB cable, you plug a digital camera into a computer and import or capture video clips. The video software has drop-down menus with built-in capture functions. You can use the camera as a playback deck; some software even allows you to control the camera remotely from the computer screen during the importing process. These programs also bring in still pictures and graphics.

To import analog images, a video capture card converts the analog information into digital data. However, since clips from a digital camera begin their lives as data, they do not require a capture card when importing.

Each piece of video is stored as a clip that can be placed on a timeline to indicate where in the finished program it will appear. At this stage, it is possible to edit and move clips, adjust the audio volume, alter the color, and add graphics. Two advantages of digital video are that it is *nonlinear* and *nondestructive.* Film and analog videotape are linear formats: One image appears after another in a distinct order. To add or delete a shot or sequence, all the film images must be shifted around to make room for the change. On the other hand, the video clips loaded into a computer are *nonlinear.* There is no beginning, middle, or end; there is only data. During the editing process, you can decide which segments to play and when to play them; these decisions are stored in the command files of the editing software. You can easily change the shot order at any time and restructure the video quickly. With a few key commands, the software will look elsewhere for the next video segment.

Nondestructive editing means that you can change and alter a sequence or program without losing anything. Video editing programs include cut and paste functions similar to those used in word processing. However, after a video segment has been added, eliminating it from the final program does not necessarily make it disappear. The software simply instructs the computer to skip over that data during playback. A new software command will restore a shot. With each alteration, there are changes in software commands, but no video is lost. Nonlinear and nondestructive editing software translate into creative freedom. You can conveniently move a video clip from location to location on the timeline to see where it fits best. Or you can decide not to include it at all.

Once the final program is assembled, you can export it to tape, burn it onto DVD, or export it as a file for other uses. If the program is to be displayed on the Web, used in a multimedia presentation, or stored on DVD, it must be converted into the appropriate format. Some choices are AVI (Audio Video Interleave), WMV (Windows Media Video), MPEG-2 (Motion Pictures Experts Group format 2), MPEG-4 (Motion Picture Experts Group format 4), RealVideo, and QuickTime.

Why are there so many formats? Manufacturers have created products or outlets with their own proprietary formats. In addition, some display options (downloading, Webcasting, multimedia, and even DVDs) limit how much data can be sent, transferred, or processed in a given time or stored in a finite space. These restrictions created a need to reduce the overall quantity of data or increase the speed with which it can be sent or transferred from one place to another. As a result, other formats were created to make these options possible.

VIDEO RECORDING

A film is made up of individual still photographs on a linear reel projected or flashed on a movie screen twenty-four times each second. Because our eyes retain these images briefly, we do not perceive the flickering as one picture being replaced by another. Instead, we see each photograph replaced with a slightly different one, which we cognitively interpret as movement. Video recording employs the same technique though the photographs are electronic images created line by line on a television screen. The National Television System Committee (NTSC) video standard used in the United States includes thirty frames (individual pictures) per second; each frame is composed of 525 lines of resolution (of which, we only see 480 on the screen). Each complete frame or picture is actually made up of two *fields.* One field includes the information from the odd lines (one, three, five, etc.) of the picture, and the other is made up of the information from the even lines (two, four, six, etc.). This is called *interlaced* scanning.

Just as a microphone converts sound energy into electrical energy, a video camera converts light into electrical energy for storage and reproduction. While there are a number of analog and digital recording devices in use today, all video cameras perform similar functions and are made up of three basic systems: a lens, an imaging device, and a viewfinder. The lens enables you to select and focus on a subject. The imaging device is a group of components that converts light into an electronic signal. The viewfinder enables you to see and review what you are recording while in the field.

Though all cameras include these three basic systems, not all cameras are equal in quality. Consumer, prosumer, and professional gear vary in price, utility, and quality.

The consumer gear you will find in electronics stores tends to be inexpensive, conveniently small, and easy to use. Most functions are automatically controlled. However, there is a trade-off for size, price, and convenience. Consumer camcorders produce lesser-quality images as a result of compromises made in each of the three basic systems.

The media industries use professional gear. The high-quality lenses, imaging devices, and viewfinders are large, heavy, and expensive. The cameras offer both manual and automatic controls, so you can adjust the focus and iris (the size of the opening that controls the amount of light passing through the lens). These manual options give you maximum control over the shots being recorded, but the clusters of buttons and switches may be confusing. Professional camcorders are durable and have long-lasting batteries.

The middle ground is the prosumer gear. The cameras are better than consumer versions but not as good as the professional equipment. They are still light, comparatively easy to use, and moderately priced. They may also have manual and automatic control choices. Documentary and news producers use this high-end consumer gear because it is a relatively cost-effective option for gathering good images.

The camera lens is one indication of quality. Expensive cameras have lenses that produce clear, sharp images and adjust smoothly as they zoom in from a wide angle to a close-up. The component parts of the imaging device are another indication of quality. Here, a beam splitter and chip receive an image from the lens and process it for recording.

Reflected and projected light follow different rules of physics. When we see a rainbow, we see seven distinct colors. These are the classic ROY-G-BIV colors: red, orange, yellow, green, blue, indigo, and violet. We look at a wall and see blue because the paint absorbs all of the wavelengths of light except blue, which is reflected back to us. A black wall absorbs all wavelengths of light, while a white one reflects all of them. This is called the subtractive system of light.

Projected light, however, operates in the additive system. If we send a beam of white light through a prism, it will separate

Characteristics of Consumer, Prosumer, and Professional Video Equipment	
Consumer	Lighter, more automatic functions Inexpensive, which may mean compromises in overall image quality May be the most fragile and least durable option
Prosumer	Heavier and more expensive Better image quality May allow for manual and automatic control functions
Professional	Heaviest and most expensive Better and smoother operating lenses Best image quality Settings for both automatic and manual control More complicated to operate Better audio system Heavier and longer-lasting batteries

into the seven colors of the rainbow. If we combine each of the seven colors in equal amounts, we will end up with white light. Black, then, is the absence of light. In theory, a camera should be capable of storing and reproducing each of the seven rainbow colors. Because this would be complex and expensive, physicists discovered a simpler way to accomplish this task. As a result, it is possible to create white light by combining the three primary colors of red, green, and blue (RGB) light. This makes the technology of the camera simpler because we can now recreate all the colors of the rainbow by recording and reproducing only three primary colors.

There are several methods of converting light into an electrical signal. Professional camcorders employ a system of prisms and filters to divide a single image into separate RGB images. These three individual images are sent to pickup devices where they are scanned and recorded. Each pickup is a chip or charge-coupled device (CCD) that consists of hundreds of thousands of individual light-sensing elements called *pixels*.

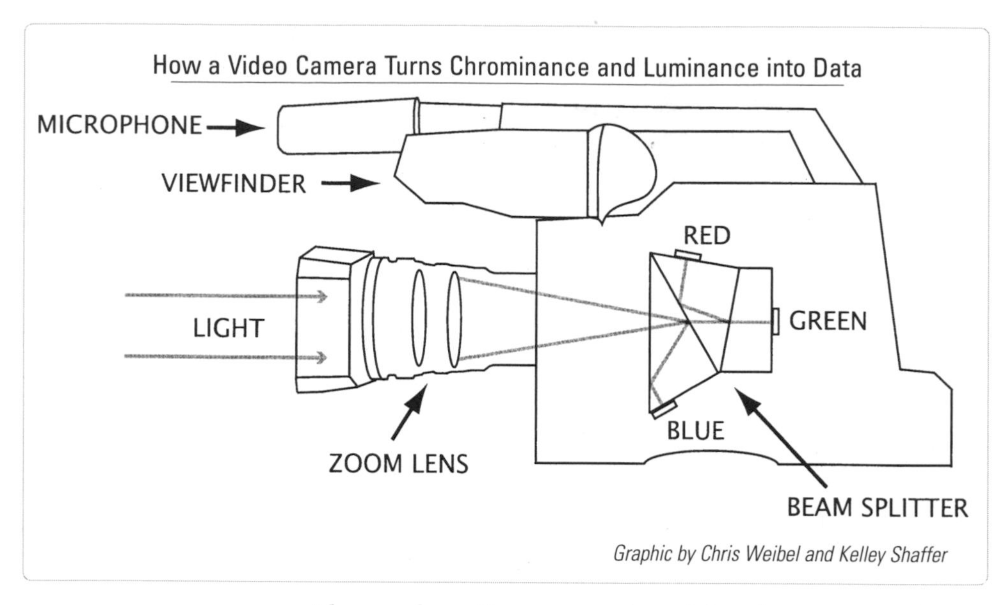

Graphic by Chris Weibel and Kelley Shaffer

The word *pixel* is a contraction of the phrase *picture element,* and it signifies the smallest component part of an image. Like dots per inch (dpi) on a computer printer, the number of pixels used to create a picture determines the detail or resolution. In video, each pixel on a CCD measures the amount of light and converts the information into an electrical charge that is measured and stored as data. Every frame of video includes data from all of the pixels and each of the three CCDs stored as color (chrominance) and black-and-white (luminance) information.

A camera's ability to reproduce color is related to the prisms, filters, and CCDs. The highest-quality cameras have three CCDs to record RGB information. An image's clarity or detail is influenced by the number of pixels found on each CCD. Some cameras employ hundreds of thousands or millions of pixels to do the job. High-definition video cameras, for instance, record images with three high-resolution CCDs, which include more lines of resolution (720 or 1,080) than the traditional NTSC image and more pixels per line, which thus improves picture clarity and color.

Consumer camcorders tend to use striped or mosaic RGB filters and a single-chip CCD to do the same job. The result is a less-expensive camera with a lower-quality image. This video information and audio data take up a lot of memory. A general rule of thumb is that a five-minute, full-quality AVI video file will require approximately 1 gigabyte (GB) of memory. There are several ways to reduce the amount of data storage needed.

One is video *compression,* which either reduces the size of the screen image or the overall quality of the images being sent perhaps by decreasing the number of pixels in each frame. Examples of software using these approaches include QuickTime, RealVideo, and Windows Media Video.

Another approach is to completely scan and record one frame of video and, for the next several frames, send only the information describing the differences between the first and subsequent frames. For example, if a person is running in front of a white wall, only the data about the runner would change while the information about the white wall would essentially remain the same. This results in a reduction or rearrangement of picture data with more efficient storage and data transfer options. DVDs, for instance, employ the MPEG-2 standard, which is able to reduce video information by as much as thirty times while still preserving a relatively high picture quality.

Again, different files that may use different compression methods are required for each distribution or display format. Broadcast television, cable television, multimedia presentations, the Internet, DVDs, and Blu-ray discs may all require files specific to that application. As a result, the project goals, funding, and distribution options should determine the choice of equipment.

Files and formats are in a state of flux as design engineers try to squeeze more data through increasingly sophisticated equipment and as the Internet becomes the medium for increased data transmission. In the future, the Web will be able to handle more data and thus less-compressed and higher-resolution

Questions to Consider When Purchasing Equipment

Who will be in charge of this equipment?

- It is important for the equipment manager to have the time, space, technical skill, and financial resources to purchase, operate, and maintain this gear.

How many people will likely use this equipment?

- All operators should have the technical skills necessary to use the equipment or the training available to do so.
- If there are many operators, things will get broken more often.

How sophisticated will the equipment be?

- Do not purchase gear that nobody understands or has time to figure out.

How heavy will the gear be?

- Small, very young, and aging individuals may not be able to carry bulky and heavy gear.

How will the recordings be used?

- High-end equipment is not needed if all the recordings will end up in a compressed format on the Internet.

How much equipment do you need?

- There is probably a difference between what you want and what you need.

What is your budget?

- It is always best to first purchase what is absolutely essential to accomplish the task at hand.

video. When that time comes, Web video will begin to look more like broadcast video does today.

Getting good recordings requires not only adequate gear but also some understanding of how to get the most out of it. It also requires vigilance, attention to detail, and a bit of creativity. The machines to do these jobs are changing and evolving, and new delivery systems are emerging on an ongoing basis. Many researchers get involved in oral history because they love the topics at hand or the contact with people, but technology issues, for better or worse, are an essential component of recording and preservation, too. As a result, sorting through the scramble of acronyms and numbers is worth the time and effort, especially when a good, clear narrative is the result.

BIBLIOGRAPHY

Alten, S. *Audio in Media*. 8th ed. Belmont, CA: Thompson Wadsworth, 2008.

Bradley, K., ed. *Guidelines on the Production and Preservation of Digital Audio Objects.* Aarhus, Denmark: International Association of Sound and Audiovisual Archives, 2004.

"Digital Audio Best Practices: Version 2.1." Collaborative Digitization Program, Digital Audio Working Group, October 2006. http://www.bcr.org/cdp/best/digital-audio-bp.pdf (accessed August 20, 2007).

"Go Digital: Turn LPs, Tapes, Photos, and Home Movies into CDs, DVDs, or Computer Files." *Consumer Reports,* June 2007, 26–29.

Levine, M. "Better Safe than Sorry." *Electronic Musician,* May 2006, 39–40, 42, 44, 46, 48–49.

Norton, P.A. "Recording the Spoken Word." *Electronic Musician,* February 2007, 33–34, 36, 38, 40–41.

Peterson, G. "Hard Disk Drives: Issues and Answers for Recording New Media." *Mix Magazine,* August 2006, 32, 34, 36.

"Planning a Digital Project." Washington State Library, Digital Best Practices. http://digitalwa.statelib.wa.gov/newsite/best.htm (accessed August 10, 2007).

Schuller, D., ed. *The Safeguarding of the Audio Heritage: Ethics, Principles, and Preservation Strategy*. Aarhus, Denmark: International Association of Sound and Audiovisual Archives, 2005.

Smithers, B. "A Musician's Guide to Digital Video." *Electronic Musician,* May 2007, 78, 80.

Zettl, H. *Television Production Handbook.* 9th ed. Belmont, CA: Thomson Wadsworth, 2006.

Chapter Eight

Audio and Video Recording

By David H. Mould and Charles F. Ganzert

Learning how to use audio and video equipment can be a frustrating experience. First impressions are important—and if these are of a confusing array of controls and flashing lights, the *technology* may seem to be a hurdle. Unfortunately, that's how audio and video recording is often presented at training sessions. The oral historian is initiated into the mysteries of scrolling through menu options on digital audio recorders, connecting AC power adaptors and cables, recharging batteries, and loading tapes. These rites of passage completed, the oral historian is sent into the field. This reduces the production process to a practical skill acquired with about the same training needed to change a fuse or an oil filter.

Audio and video are not only skills but also languages capable of capturing the range of human emotions. A good-quality audio recording will convey the tone, pitch, rhythm, and character of voice, elements that are often lost in a poor-quality recording. Video places the interviewee in an environment and shows size, shape, color, texture, and facial expressions. To produce good-quality audio and video, you need not only practical skills but also creativity and the ability to adapt to any situation.

The Nighthawk Throws a Curveball

By Charles F. Ganzert

Some time ago, I produced a series of radio documentaries called *'Tis Sweet to Be Remembered* that featured the stories and songs of early radio performers and country music pioneers. One was Lee Moore, an all-night radio personality on WWVA in Wheeling, West Virginia, who was known as the Coffee-Drinking Nighthawk. Lee told stories and sang songs to an audience of truck drivers, mechanics, and late-shift factory workers. He kept a special sound effects microphone at hand that enabled him to brew a pot of coffee, pour out a cup, add cream and sugar, and stir it on the air as he talked.

I had driven a long way to Lee's home in Albany, New York, and expected the interview to focus on his long career in the radio industry. I was surprised when, after we had got to know each other, Lee took out his guitar, a songbook, and a music stand, and put on his cowboy hat. Within a few seconds, it became clear that Lee had no intention of discussing old radio; he planned to do it, right there in the living room.

As luck would have it, I had brought several extra microphones, cables, and stands, and I was using a stereo recorder with separate inputs for the right and left channels. I put a microphone on Lee and another on his guitar, and I sent these two signals separately into the two channels of the stereo recorder. This is called *split-track* recording; it requires recording separate signals on channel one (left) and channel two (right) and later mixing them together.

For several hours, the Coffee-Drinking Nighthawk talked and sang some of his favorite old songs. The combination of performance and interview captured the sound and spirit of old radio in a way that an interview or a single-microphone recording could never have done. That's why it's important to have extra equipment (microphones, cables, stands, and recording media) on hand. Some opportunities present themselves unexpectedly, and they shouldn't be missed.

Long after his radio career was over, Lee Moore, the "Coffee-Drinking Nighthawk," continued performing. Here, he rehearses for the 1983 WWVA radio Wheeling Jamboree.
Courtesy of Charles F. Ganzert

You can also use the split-track approach to record two voices—the interviewer and interviewee or two interviewees. The voices are recorded on separate tracks that are later mixed to the proper levels. You can also use the technique when interviewing someone whose voice level fluctuates significantly. An editor can locate and piece together all the parts of the interview that are recorded at optimal levels to create a final narrative that sounds natural and appropriate.

Split-Track Recording Technique

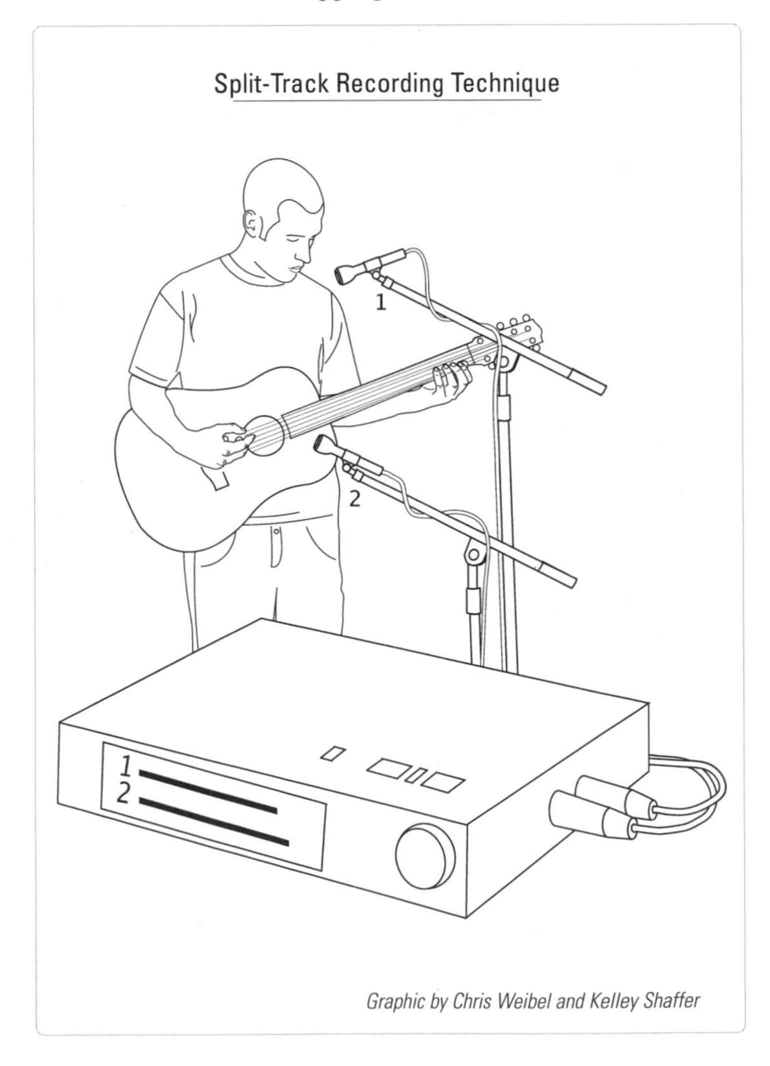

Graphic by Chris Weibel and Kelley Shaffer

MICROPHONE PLACEMENT

For most interviews, there are three choices: holding the microphone, placing it on a stand, or using a lapel (clip-on) microphone.

The main advantage to holding the microphone is that you can easily move around. If the interviewee is showing you around his farm or workshop, you need to be able to follow him. The best technical option is a wireless lapel microphone, but these are relatively expensive and require a small transmitter and receiver. An ordinary lapel microphone may work if the area of movement is limited, but it leaves the interviewee precariously tethered by a cable to your recorder. When you need to move during an interview, use a directional microphone (one that reduces the level of environmental sound or noise). Wrap a handkerchief or soft cloth around the body of the microphone to reduce handling noise.

In a static interview situation, try not to hold the microphone. It's difficult to keep it steady, even when you brace your arm against a solid object. When the microphone moves, the level and presence of the interviewee's voice will change. Then there's the issue of social space. It takes tact, grace, and technique to comfortably locate yourself within a person's personal space. An interviewee will likely not be troubled by a microphone on a small stand placed several inches away from his or her face; however, you may come off as pushy if you start shoving a handheld microphone close to the person's face.

The microphone should be within four to six inches of the interviewee and pointed at—but not directly in front of—the mouth. The best way to do this is to use a tabletop, boom, vertical, or gooseneck microphone stand. Although a stand is another piece of gear to carry, it helps you place the microphone close to the interviewee while staying outside the zone of personal space. Tabletop stands are conveniently small, but make sure that the interviewee does not tap on the stand or pound the table to make a point. These unwanted sounds will be transferred through the stand to the microphone and become part of the recording. You can offset this somewhat by placing a mouse pad, soft cloth, or carpet remnant beneath the stand.

Gooseneck and straight stands rest on the floor, so they tend to solve the tabletop issue of potentially transmitting un-

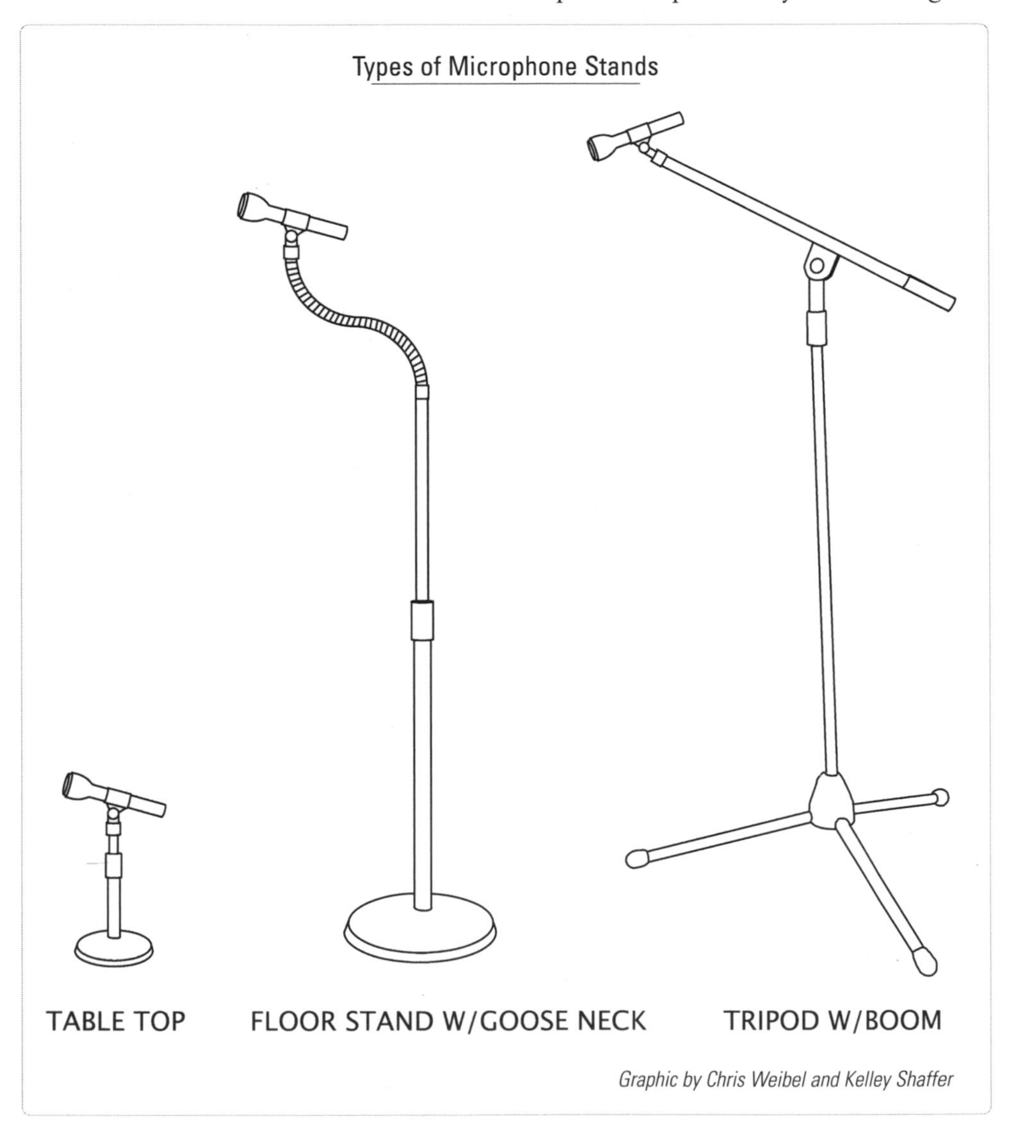

Graphic by Chris Weibel and Kelley Shaffer

wanted sound. However, they can get in the way of a table and chairs and thus are not always practical. A boom is the largest microphone stand, but it has the advantage of being able to reach over a table or large chair to hold the microphone in the proper position.

Room acoustics are another issue. A microphone placed close to a person speaking will minimize the reflected sounds in a room. Conversely, as a microphone is moved away, more and more reflected sounds are included. Reflected sounds can provide a sense of atmosphere or location, but they also affect intelligibility as they compete with or muddy the voice recording.

Placing a microphone too close to the interviewee's mouth can produce distracting pops and hisses. The pops result from *plosive* sounds (words with B, P, T, and D) and the hisses from *sibilant* sounds (words with F, S, C, H, and Z). The microphone measures changes in air pressure, and these sounds produce more signal than it can handle. One way to avoid plosives and sibilants is to place a foam pop filter over the head of the microphone, but this may also obstruct the sound waves and make the microphone less sensitive. Another approach is to place the microphone away from the plosive and sibilant sounds. While keeping the microphone four to six inches away from the interviewee, position it at a forty-five-degree angle to one side but still pointed at the mouth. The abrupt changes in air pressure will pass by the diaphragm of the microphone. Make sure the interviewee does not turn to directly face the microphone—a common impulse. The third option is to place the microphone at a forty-five-degree angle above the interviewee's mouth so that plosive sounds pass under the diaphragm. Again, people are tempted to raise their heads to face the microphone, and sometimes the microphone and cable may become a visual obstruction.

Some interviewers clip a lapel microphone to the interviewee's clothing a few inches below the person's head. There

Microphone Positions to Avoid Pops and Hisses

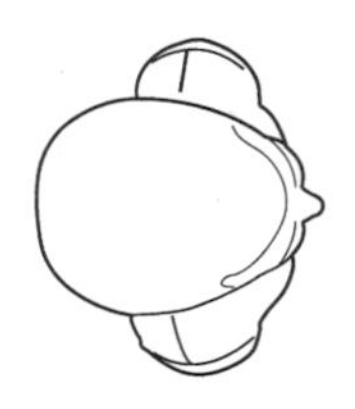

Same height as the mouth, but 45 degrees to one side and pointed directly at the mouth. Pops pass by the microphone but not directly at it.

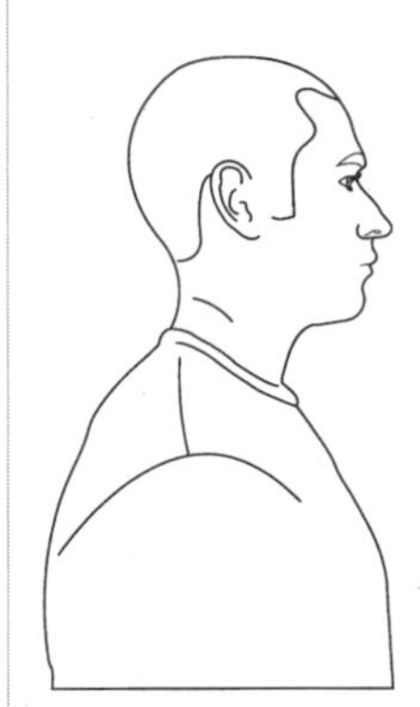

Above the speaker's mouth and pointed downward directly at the mouth. Pops pass under the microphone, but not directly at it.

Graphic by Chris Weibel and Kelley Shaffer

are two main advantages to doing this: The microphone is less conspicuous than a hand-held or stand-held microphone and thus may put the interviewee at ease, and it will always be at the same distance from the interviewee's mouth. However, a lapel microphone and its cable are sensitive to transmitted noise and may pick up rustling sounds as the interviewee shifts position. You can prevent this by making sure the microphone is firmly clipped to the person's clothing and that the cable does not hang loose.

Where you place the microphone affects signal levels—that is, the loudness of the recording. If the microphone is too close to an interviewee, the sound levels can cause *over-modulation,* the distortion created by an incoming signal that is stronger than the recording machine can handle. You need to use meters or

LED displays to adjust the input so that the signal is not too loud or too quiet.

Some devices have an automatic gain control that allows the recording machine itself to set the proper recording level. Others enable you to adjust the level manually. Digital recorders have a tendency to distort quickly after the signal exceeds the appropriate level, which is usually labeled "0 VU." For recorders that require manual adjustment, keep the recording at or below this mark even during the loud portions of the interview. It is usually best to set the level so that the meter peaks in the minus ten (–10 VU) to fifteen (–15 VU) range. To do this, test the levels before the interview begins. Some people become nervous and speak louder once the actual recording begins,

Listening to the Room

By David H. Mould

In my days as a radio feature producer, I developed the habit of listening to the room. I walk into a room, close the door, and then stand silently for a few minutes listening for sounds in the environment. That's when I notice the hum of a fluorescent light, the rattle of a screen door, or the whirring sound of a fan or computer. Even rooms that seem quiet often have a high level of ambient noise, particularly in modern office buildings with heating and air-conditioning systems. Human hearing is highly selective, and we easily ignore these sounds in a normal conversation. But the microphone doesn't discriminate between wanted and unwanted sounds.

You cannot avoid unexpected sounds—a car arriving, a dog barking, the phone ringing. But you can avoid locations where the background sound is not related to the interview and interferes with understanding. Those few moments of listening to the room may be time well spent when it comes to listening to, transcribing, or editing the interview. It may seem like a good idea to interview the Polish community leader while the All-Star Polka Band rips it up onstage, but you'll find it more difficult to focus on what the interviewee was saying later. If you edit interview sections together, the band will miss much more than a beat.

Avoid rhythmic background sound whenever possible. Once I edited an interview recorded in a living room with a clock rhythmically ticking in the background. At almost every edit point, I had to pay attention not only to what the interviewee was saying, but also to the rhythm of the clock. Often I had to insert short pauses to restore its rhythm and avoid an annoying tick . . . tock . . . tick...tick. My job was to edit the interview into a radio feature, but I spent just as much time editing the clock.

so it may be necessary to readjust the recording level during the interview.

Wearing headphones is the best way to know how a recording is going. Headphones make it easy to identify plosives, sibilants, and hand noises by listening to the signal as it is being recorded. It is also easier to adjust the equipment during the session—for example, by moving a microphone—than to try to cut noises from the recording later. Some machines allow you to select whether to listen to the signal before or after it has been recorded. Checking the actual recording during the session helps to confirm that the machine is working properly.

THERE'S NO PLACE LIKE HOME

If the interview is at the interviewee's home, which room is best? Avoid the kitchen (even though this is the most common place for conversation) because it is usually a high-traffic area and has hard, reflective surfaces that make the sound bounce around, giving it a distant, echo-like quality. And then there's Acoustic Enemy Number One: the refrigerator. It may be silent when you start the interview, but at some point the compressor motor will kick on and put out a low, annoying drone. The living room is a better choice. Soft furnishings and drapes absorb sound; there should be few distracting sounds once the TV is turned off. The problem is deciding where you and the interviewee will sit, a question of appropriate social distance. Assuming you don't sit next to each other on the couch—a friendly but unprofessional position—you'll likely end up in an armchair across the room from the interviewee. That may put you several feet away and create problems in microphone placement. If you need to move the furniture to bring yourself closer to the interviewee, explain that you're doing so to improve the sound quality.

Howard Sacks recommends interviewing in the dining room, which is often the least-used room in the house and usually has

What's the best place to conduct an interview? An interviewee usually prefers talking at home and will often invite the interviewer to sit at the kitchen table. The kitchen is a comfortable, familiar setting but has potential problems—family members walking in and out, hard, reflective surfaces, and noise from the refrigerator. *Courtesy of the Rural Life Center, Kenyon College*

no phone or television. It has drapes and sound-absorbent surfaces. The interviewee can sit comfortably at the head of the table while you sit to the left or right at an angle across the table with the recorder between you. Cover the part of the table where you are conducting the interview with a cloth to reduce reflections. The dining room is familiar and comfortable for the interviewee yet a bit more formal—very appropriate for an interview.

Some interviewers feel awkward about asking an interviewee to move to another room or about rearranging the furniture. In our experience, most interviewees will understand if you explain you need to do this to improve the sound quality. It's better to have a brief moment of awkwardness than an interview that is difficult to listen to, transcribe, or edit. There are limits to interview preparation, of course. Don't arrive armed with acoustic baffles and duct tape, ready to transform a room into a recording studio. But do walk through the house to select the best room, move furniture, and put a cloth on a table to show that you're taking the job seriously.

Set up your equipment in full view of the interviewee, and explain what you're doing. In other words, demystify the technology. There may still be a few purists who believe that technology is intrusive and that you should try to conceal or ignore it. Such scruples may satisfy the conscience, but they result in horrible recordings. Let's be honest: The interviewee knows that you are recording the interview, so you should not apologize for your equipment. Some oral historians show interviewees how to use the recorder and have them record their own voice and play it back through headphones. It's most important to build rapport between interviewer and interviewee, but a little rapport with technology also helps.

WHY USE VIDEO FOR ORAL HISTORY?

If your answer to this question is "Because we have money to buy video equipment," you're not using it for the right reason. Aside from the (still important) issues of funds, resources, and staff production skills, the choice of video over audio should be determined by the *topic* of your oral history project and/or how you plan to *distribute* or *exhibit* the interviews to an audience. If you're making a documentary for a local TV station, planning to stream video on the Web, or designing a visually interactive museum exhibit, then the choice is obvious. However, some organizations launch video oral history projects without a clear idea of why they are using the medium.

The next question to ask is, "What can video provide that audio can't?" If you can't answer that question convincingly, then, again, you probably should not be using video. However, video is the medium of choice for some topics. How can you capture the inspiration of a visual artist without showing images of his or her paintings? A quilter without images of quilts?

A historic preservationist without images of threatened buildings? An environmental activist without images of polluted streams or mountaintop removal? Video can reveal aspects that may be invisible—or, at least, difficult to describe—in audio, including:

- size, shape, color, form, texture
- interviewee's physical environment
- spatial relationships
- body language and human emotions

THE LANGUAGE OF VIDEO

Oral history interviews with inept camerawork and unimaginative framing can make even the most interesting interviewee look pretty dull. There's no excuse for this. People who view video interviews invariably place them in the context of their own media experiences, and these are defined by years of television and movie viewing. We're not suggesting oral history interviews with sweeping camera movements and fast cuts; let's leave the flashy stuff where it belongs (not in oral history). But that doesn't mean you should go to the other extreme and leave the camera on a static wide shot for the whole interview. You should use the creative language of video to enhance the oral history interview to make it more meaningful for the viewer. The body language of an interview subject may reinforce or contradict what he or she is saying; if you do *not* show a facial expression, you may indeed be depriving the interview of some of its significance.

We need to go beyond the mere *technology* of video—what all the knobs and buttons do—to make intelligent use of the medium. To do this, we must develop a visual vocabulary. We need to know how to frame shots of our interviewees and the things they talk about. The camera is a tool for selective vision—it sees only what we decide to show it. This may seem an obvious point, but it's worth stressing. The camera cannot match the eye's perspective; it sees only one thing at a time. It's up to us to make what it sees as interesting as possible.

Screen Size and Aspect Ratio

Whatever you shoot, it's likely to end up on a television or computer screen. When you think of either screen, think small. Despite recent consumer demand for large-screen TVs, most people still watch TV on screens of twenty-six inches or less. The sweeping landscape shot, impressive to the eye, doesn't look nearly as impressive on the small screen. TV shows detail best. So while you can use a wide shot to establish an interview location, shoot your subject with medium views and close views to capture the facial expressions that are less obvious in a wide shot.

When film directors look at potential shots through a rectangle formed by their thumbs and index fingers, they're trying to see a shot the way the audience will see it. The standard TV screen has a fixed aspect ratio of 4:3—four units wide by three units high—that limits its visual potential. This gives it a horizontal orientation close to our normal field of vision. The arrival of high-definition television (HDTV) has not changed this; its aspect ratio is 16:9, which makes it even more horizontal in orientation. While it's easy to frame horizontal objects, vertical ones—tall people, tall buildings—don't fit as well. You have to move so far away from the subject that you lose detail, cut off part of it to make it fit the frame, or shoot it from an unusual angle below or above the normal eyeline.

Field of View

The lens is the camera's eye. Its focal length determines the camera's field of view—how far it can see to left and right. In the case of a *normal lens,* this range is about twenty-five degrees. The normal lens approximates the perspective of the human eye; objects seen through the viewfinder appear at the same size and distance and in the same proportion as those seen with the eye. By contrast, a short lens shows a wider area than the normal twenty-five degrees—hence the name *wide-angle lens;* a long or *telephoto lens* shows a narrower area. When you move to the wide-angle or telephoto position on a zoom lens, the field of view changes. These lenses have other characteristics that change the image the camera sees:

1. Because the wide-angle lens includes a larger area than the normal lens at the same distance, it's good for shooting in cramped places where you can't move the camera any farther back. The telephoto lens includes a smaller area than the normal lens, so it's good for shooting distant subjects when you can't move the camera closer.
2. The wide-angle lens makes the subject appear smaller in the frame than it would if you were using the normal lens at the same distance; the telephoto lens makes the subject appear larger than it would if you were using the normal lens at the same distance.
3. The wide-angle lens exaggerates depth and makes subjects appear farther apart than normal; the telephoto lens compresses depth and makes them appear closer together than normal. The wide-angle lens spreads out the features of a subject's face; the telephoto lens flattens and compresses them.
4. The small image size of the wide-angle lens makes camera jiggles less noticeable, so if you can't use a tripod, stay in the wide-angle position. Conversely, the larger image size of the telephoto lens makes camera jiggles more noticeable.

Headroom and Talkspace

When you shoot an interview, it's important to place the interviewee in a comfortable position within the four-by-three frame. There are two elements here—*headroom* and *talkspace* (or *eyeroom*). *Headroom* is the distance between the top of a person's head and the top edge of the frame. If there's too little headroom, the person appears to stick to the top of the frame; if there's too much, the person appears to be sinking out of the frame. There's no formula for calculating headroom, but you need more on wide shots and less on close-ups. Pay attention to headroom if you zoom in or zoom out. As you zoom in and the interviewee's head becomes larger, the headroom will decrease, and you may need to tilt up to correct the framing. As you zoom out and the head becomes smaller, headroom will increase, and you may have to tilt down to compensate. *Talkspace,* or *eyeroom,* refers to the distance from the side of the speaker's face to the edge of the screen. The direction a person faces creates a powerful force in the frame, and this needs to be balanced in the composition of the picture. If there is too little space, the interviewee seems boxed in with no room to talk; too much space may be unsettling, too.

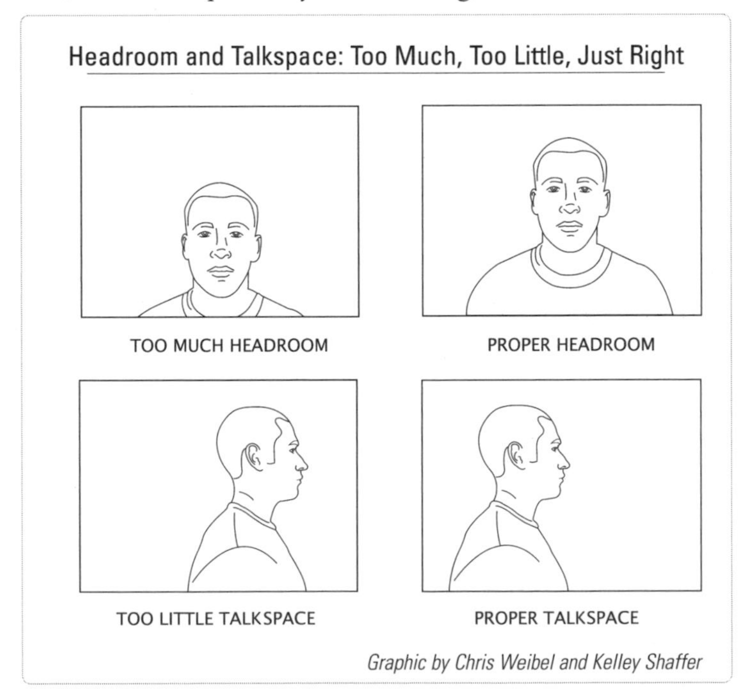

Graphic by Chris Weibel and Kelley Shaffer

The Rule of Thirds

Divide the picture frame into thirds, horizontally and vertically, and place important picture elements at the intersection of the lines.

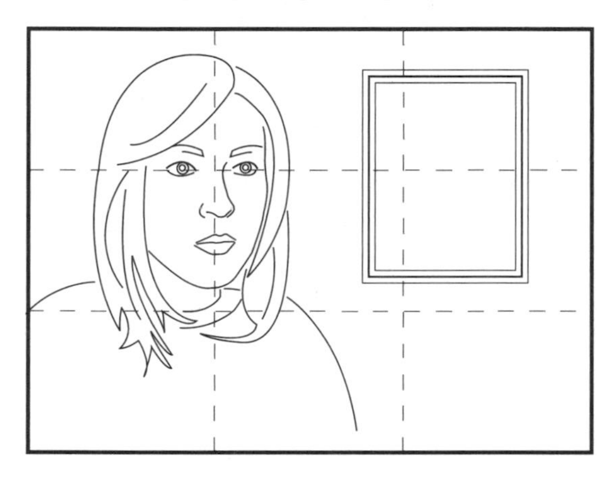

Graphic by Chris Weibel and Kelley Shaffer

The Rule of Thirds

There's a common tendency to place the most important element—the interviewee's face—smack in the middle of the frame. That works fine for a TV news anchor talking directly to the camera, but it's not the best way to shoot an interview. The interviewee is talking to an interviewer—not the camera—and thus should be looking screen left or screen right. One useful guideline for framing the interview shot is the rule of thirds. Mentally divide the TV screen into thirds both vertically and horizontally, and place the points of interest—the eyes and the mouth—at or near the intersection of the lines. This composition will produce a more interesting and pleasing image than centering the face in the frame.

Natural Dividing Lines

The human body has natural divisions at the neck, the waist, and the knees. Do not frame a person so that the bottom edge of the frame lines up with one of these divisions. Such framing appears to detach the person from the rest of his or her body. Conversely, if you frame with a head-and-shoulders shot that cuts off just below the shoulders or with a three-quarters shot that cuts off just above the knees, the viewer will mentally complete the picture. You can even cut off the top and bottom of the head with an eyes and mouth shot. It's a bit intense and melodramatic—you often see this shot in confessional interview sequences on TV—but it works well as composition.

Depth and Angles

The screen has only two dimensions—height and width. You can give a sense of depth by shooting at an angle so the viewer can see at least two sides of the subject. Shooting only the front of a building makes it look flat; shooting at an angle that shows part of the front and one side gives it depth. The same goes for the interviewee: Shooting the person in profile makes the picture look flat and results in the infamous ear shot. Changing the angle to show more of the face results in a more pleasing three-quarters shot that has depth and reveals more facial features.

Eye Level

Place the camera at the interviewee's eye level. This neutral, objective position that keeps the viewer and interviewee on the same level is used in most news, documentary, and interview shots. Placing the camera either above or below the normal eye level position alters the viewer's perception. When the camera is above eye level—a *high-angle* shot—it looks down and makes the interviewee seem small, inferior, or less significant. Conversely, a position below eye level—the *low-angle* shot—makes an interviewee look more powerful, or imposing. Such shots are a visual commentary that should be avoided.

High-Angle, Low-Angle, and Eye-Level Shots

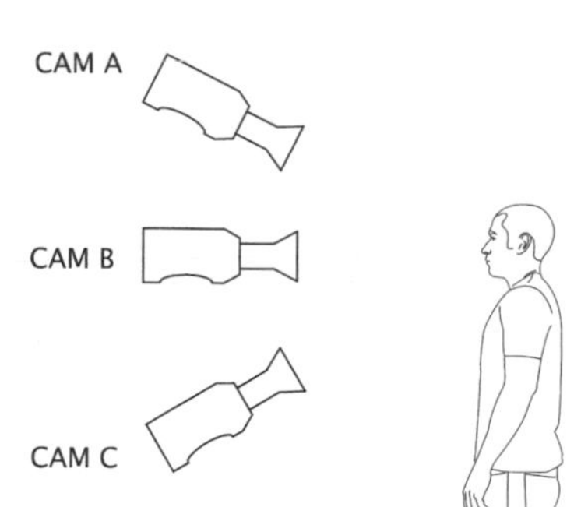

CAMERA VIEW A

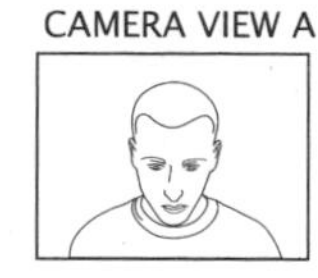

CAMERA VIEW B

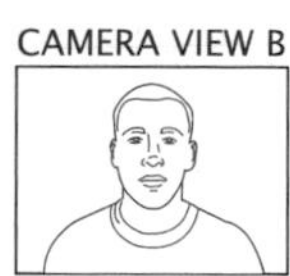

CAMERA VIEW C

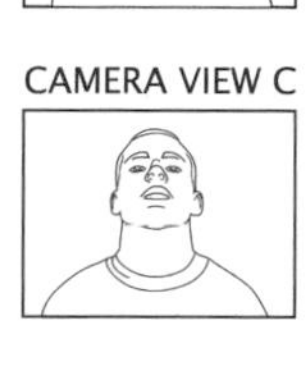

A: A high-angle shot looks down on the subject and implies that the subject is less powerful than the camera/audience.

B: An eye-level shot implies that the camera/audience and subject are equal.

C: A low-angle shot looks up at the subject and implies that the subject is more powerful than the camera/audience.

Graphic by Chris Weibel and Kelley Shaffer

Backgrounds

The best background is the one that stays where it belongs—in the background. There are few things more distracting in an interview than a background that diverts attention from the interviewee. The most common kinds of distracting backgrounds are

1. Objects that appear to grow out of the interviewee's head. Don't frame an interview shot with a door frame, window, tree, or pole behind the interviewee.

2. Backgrounds that are visually busy with details and colors that overwhelm the subject. A vivid canvas may crowd out the artist; the office bulletin board may distract attention from the person behind the desk.
3. Unusual or persistent movements in the background—people talking or waving to the camera, passing cars and trucks.

If you can't remove the distraction—by moving the interviewee or changing the shot—leave the background out of focus. This technique, known as *selective focus,* makes the interviewee the center of interest in the frame and the background deliberately indistinct. To do this, use the telephoto position with a short depth of field.

Camera and Lens Movements

There's a tendency, particularly among beginners, to keep moving the camera—to zoom in and out, pan left and right, tilt up and down. Unnecessary movements not only are distracting, but also call attention to the camera. It is no longer the invisible observer of the scene, but part of it. A camera move should have a purpose and thus contribute to the viewer's understanding. If it doesn't, it's not worth doing. There are three types of camera movements:

1. *The Zoom.* The zoom lens has variable focal length. It was developed to allow the camera operator to set up shots without changing lenses. The zoom brings the scene closer to or pushes it further away from the viewer. The zoom can be effective when it is used properly, but there must be a reason for it; zooming in and out to add movement to a scene is bad practice and nauseating to the viewer. The *zoom-in* from wide shot to close-up should direct attention to something—a facial expression, a detail of the scene. The *zoom-out* usually reveals new information, such as a location.

2. *Pans and Tilts.* These are camera head movements; the *pan* is a horizontal move, the *tilt* a vertical one. Again, they should have a purpose, revealing new information to the viewer. The *pan,* short for panorama, should show the length of an object or the physical relationship between two points in a scene, such as two interviewees. The *tilt* shows height or the relationship between two points in a scene. Begin and end the movement with a well-composed static shot; it can be distracting to cut from a static shot to a move that's already in progress or to cut from a move to a static shot. The move should begin and end at a point of interest in the scene; if you shoot a building, don't end up with the sky filling the screen. Panning back and forth—spraying the garden, as it's called—is as distracting as zooming in and out. Do not pan too fast; if you do, vertical lines, such as fence posts or doorframes, will strobe, trailing ghost images behind.
3. *Camera Body Movements.* These are physical movements of the camera itself. In a *dolly,* the camera is moved toward or away from the scene. A *truck* is a horizontal movement to the left or right. An *arc* is a semicircular movement around the scene. It's difficult to accomplish these movements smoothly without special equipment; trying to dolly with the camera on your shoulder is not only tiring, but is also likely to produce a very wobbly shot. These moves, like the others, should be undertaken only with a purpose. There's little reason for doing them in the oral history interview.

AN INTERVIEW SETUP

It's difficult to conduct an interview and operate a camera at the same time. The interviewer needs to concentrate on questions and answers, the cameraperson on light, framing, movement, and audio levels. We recommend a two-person crew for video interviews; two thinking heads are definitely better than one. Good communication is important; interviewer and cameraperson should discuss in advance the type of shots they want. During the interview, the cameraperson should listen attentively and visually follow the action while the interviewer focuses on content and thinks about how to phrase the next question.

Let's look at a simple interview setup, the types of shots, and some typical problems. In setting up the interview, consider these factors:

1. position of the interviewee
2. position of the interviewer
3. position of the camera
4. screen direction—the principal action axis

The interviewee should be in a comfortable position at eye level to the camera. Check the background to make sure it does not distract attention from the interviewee. There are two possible positions for the interviewer—next to the interviewee, the normal sitting position for conversation, or facing the interviewee with back to the camera. The first may make the interviewee feel more comfortable. But it will present the camera with a side shot of the face—the infamous ear shot—because the interviewee will tend to turn toward the interviewer and away from the camera. The second position presents the camera with an almost full-face shot, which is visually more pleasing. For this shot, place the camera a few feet behind the interviewer and off to one side. From this position, you can shoot a three-quarter profile of the interviewee, a close-up, and an over-the-shoulder shot of the interviewer and interviewee. Try to keep the distance between the interviewer and interviewee relatively short so that you can zoom in for a tight close-up of the subject but stay in focus when you zoom out for the over-the-shoulder shot.

If you draw a straight line from the interviewer to the interviewee and then extend it beyond both of them, you have established the *axis of action*. All shots should be taken from one side of the line; if you cross it and take shots from the other side, you will break screen direction and confuse the viewer. *Screen direction* is the direction that people and things face when viewed through the camera. If the interviewer is facing screen right and the interviewee screen left, each will keep facing the same way no matter where you put the camera on

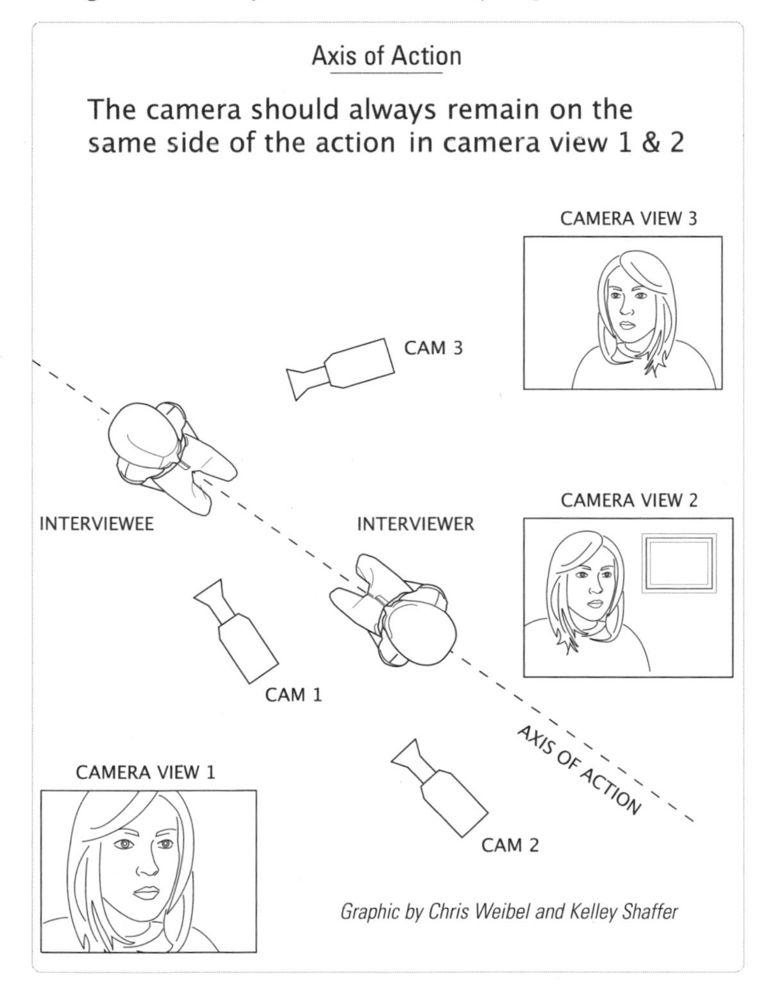

Graphic by Chris Weibel and Kelley Shaffer

one side of the line. The same rule of screen direction applies in any scene where people or objects move, or face, left or right. That's why football games are shot from one side of the field. If screen direction was reversed in a car chase scene, the cars would be set on a visual collision course.

INSERTS AND CUTAWAYS

Remember to take individual shots of objects or scenes that the interviewee mentions—from the photos in the family album and the rack of antlers over the fireplace to the farm implement, the family graveyard, or the faithful dog that saved him from the fire. Editing in these images helps you to document the narrative and provide visual variety. Such *inserts* have another important function in editing: They enable you to cut seamlessly from one part of the interview to another. When you edit together two sections of an interview, a *jump-cut* will occur as the interviewee's head position shifts slightly; inserting a different shot will cover the transition. The insert visually refers to something the interviewee is discussing. If you need to cut at another point and do not have a relevant insert, then you need a *cutaway*. This is part of the interview scene shot from a different perspective or angle: It can be a wide shot of the interviewer and interviewee, a reverse-angle shot of the interviewer listening, or a close-up shot of the interviewee's hands or a clothing detail. It's better to use an insert than a cutaway, but make sure you record enough cutaways to cover the shot changes.

LIGHTING

The Indian poet and author Rabindranath Tagore has called pictures "a memory of light treasured by the shadow."[1] A good picture, then, is created by the interplay of light and shadow. Although modern cameras can handle low light levels, a well-lit scene will always produce a better image. Lighting is just as important as framing in shooting interviews.

The best and most natural lighting source is the cheapest one—the sun. If you're shooting outside, make sure thc sun is behind the camera casting light on the interviewee's face. That's why on sunny days it's best to shoot in the early morning or late afternoon; when the sun is overhead it casts shadows on the interviewee's face. Cloudy or overcast days are better because the light levels are more even. One of the most useful lighting instruments is a reflector that you can easily make by covering a sheet of cardboard with aluminum foil. This can direct light onto the interviewee's face to brighten it or to soften shadows; it can also reduce the level of direct light when placed between the sun and the interviewee.

The second, more expensive option (but one you may need if there is no natural light) is a lighting kit. A single light that attaches to the camera body, like the one used by TV news crews, provides enough light for the camera to operate but usually makes the image of the interviewee look flat. Whenever possible, use a kit with at least three lights: a key, a fill, and a backlight.

The *key light* is the main source of illumination that stands in for the sun. It should be positioned above eye level and slightly off to one side of the camera. Proper placement will create shadows that define the nose and the contours of the face. The *fill* is a less-focused light placed on the opposite side of the interviewee but nearer the camera than the key. This reduces but does not eliminate the contrast of the dark shadows the key light creates. When locating the fill light, it is important to avoid creating a second set of shadows on the opposite side of the face. The objective is to lighten or partially fill in the existing shadows. The *backlight* is a directional light placed behind the interviewee to shine on the back of the head and shoulders. This helps to separate the person from the background. It should be positioned above eye level and not

Three-Point Lighting

KEY: the key light represents the sun. It is the main light source but may create shadows.

FILL: the fill is the second light. It reduces the darkness of shadows and contrast created by the key light.

BACK: the back light is above and behind the subject. It illuminates the back of the head and shoulders and separates the subject from the background.

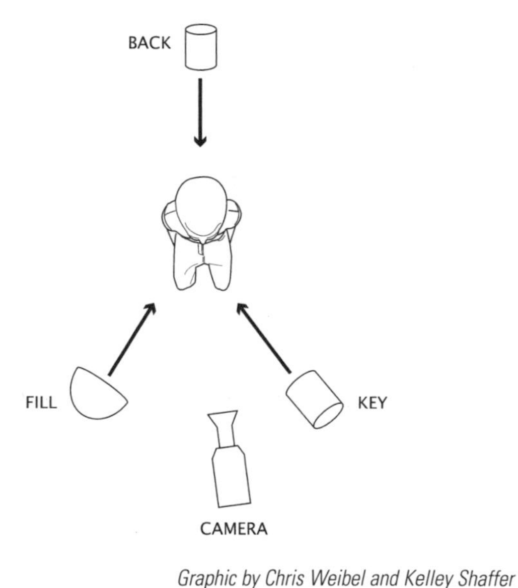

Graphic by Chris Weibel and Kelley Shaffer

pointed directly into the camera to avoid lens flares or other image problems.

DON'T FORGET THE AUDIO

It's all too easy to devote lots of effort to the picture and neglect the audio. Don't forget that images of the interview mean nothing without sound, and that tone, accent, and dialect can enrich the viewer's understanding.

Unfortunately, video equipment manufacturers often sacrifice audio quality in their efforts to provide good pictures at a reasonable price. Most camcorders come with an inexpensive unidirectional capacitor (or electret) microphone mounted on the camera body. While this can record ambient sound, it should not be used for the interview. Although the microphone is directional, it is too far away from the interviewee and will pick up background sounds. A better option is to connect an external microphone, probably a lapel microphone, to the audio input of the camera.

THE TRIPOD OF VISUAL OBJECTIVITY

Some oral historians have been reluctant to use video. Sometimes, this stems from lack of money, equipment, and trained staff. However, even those with resources have worried about the effect of the technology on the interview. Will the camera make the interviewee feel inhibited or encourage the person to show off? Will the interviewer be nervous or try to play the aggressive reporter role? In sum, does video threaten the interview's authenticity?

If there is an answer to this question, we haven't found it yet. Nevertheless, more and more oral historians are using video—if not for the interviews themselves then for supporting documentation. If they are to justify the use of video to the more skeptical members of the oral history community, then they must be careful to maintain visual objectivity—to frame shots that look natural and not contrived and, above all, to make the camera as invisible as possible. Excessive camera movements—pans, tilts, and zooms—are distracting because they draw attention to the camera's presence. That's why the most objective camera is the one on a tripod. The handheld camera, even in the firmest grasp, is unstable; when jiggling and wobbling, it is no longer invisible but part of the scene. Although the tripod may do nothing to calm the interviewee, it has a salutary effect on the camera. From this stable position, the camera can be an observer. Its function is to stand outside the scene and record what happens, not to participate in the oral history being recorded.

KEEPING TECHNOLOGY IN PERSPECTIVE

Interviewing is a demanding and tiring experience. You'll focus better on the questions and answers if you're not worrying about the technology. That means you need to be thoroughly familiar with the equipment. Before you leave for the first interview, take some time to set it up, record a sample interview, and review the results. Try out lighting approaches, microphone placement, and camera angles. Put the gear through its paces and see how it performs. Many oral historians have horror stories about forgotten batteries, cables, or connectors or about equipment letting them down. Keep a checklist of gear and make sure everything is in working order before you leave for the interview. A few minutes spent looking over the gear can save hours of frustration later.

With advances in digital technology, it's easy to get carried away by the bells and whistles of audio and video recording. Don't. As an oral historian, you're not seeking a Grammy or an Emmy nomination for special effects. You're doing an interview. Technical quality is important, but content comes first.

NOTES

1. Rabindranath Tagore, *Fireflies,* 2nd ed. (New York: Collier, 1955), 143.

Chapter Nine

Archiving Oral History

By Stephen H. Paschen

While working on an exhibit relating to local and regional amusement parks for the Summit County Historical Society (Ohio) more than two decades ago, I found primary source materials to be quite scarce. However, when I was installing the exhibit in a local shopping mall weeks later, scores of passersby stopped to view the photographs and artifacts. Many of these people shared firsthand memories of the parks with me. I realized that the scant body of primary sources I had found in repositories could be increased by preserving these people's memories. The Speaking of Summit oral history project was the result. Beginning with some of the visitors I met while installing the exhibit, I interviewed people whose lives had been touched by experiences at amusement parks. The interviewee list included descendants of former owners, ride operators, concessions workers, and, of course, the people who rode the roller coasters.

Because other sources of information were hard to find, I was mindful that by conducting oral histories I was creating and preserving primary sources that would have lasting value. Eventually, these interviews provided material for a book called *Shootin' the Chutes: Amusement Parks Remembered.*[1] The interview

Pictures evoke memories and can inspire oral history projects. When an exhibit of archival photographs of amusement parks in northeastern Ohio opened at an Akron shopping mall, people stopped by to share their memories. Lacking primary sources on the parks, the Summit County Historical Society realized that their stories could help us understand how, in the era before television, urban workers spent their leisure time. Akron's Summit Beach Park, seen here in a 1919 picture, was remembered by many interviewed for the Speaking of Summit oral history project. The interviews and transcripts, now in the University of Akron's archives, have been used by other researchers. *Courtesy of the Summit County Historical Society*

tapes and transcripts, part of the Summit County Historical Society's holdings, are housed in the climate-controlled archives of the Akron–Summit County Public Library. In later years, while employed at the archives, I was able to make the collection available to other researchers for a variety of projects.

Maybe you only want to conduct a handful of interviews for a book, an exhibit, or a radio or television production. Why worry about the long-term preservation and availability of your modest collection? There are two reasons why you might want to make sure the materials find a permanent home after your project is completed.

First, oral history literally and figuratively gives voice to history. It is the unique, direct testimony of people who experienced the past. Subject to the flaws of human memory, oral history not only documents what might not be documented in written records (which also are produced by humans who make mistakes in formally recording events), but it also directly delivers the perspective and feeling of one person at a time. Each archived interview is a primary source document that contributes a unique account for future researchers to examine and interpret.

Second, when recruiting interviewees, it is more compelling to tell each prospective interviewee that not only will his or her individual story appear in a final product such as an exhibit or television show, but it also will be preserved for posterity and available to future researchers. Oral history, in my view, verifies that each interviewee's life is significant in its own way, separate from the bigger topic, and worthy of preservation as part of history.

Archiving involves record-keeping, attention to long-term preservation, selection of an appropriate repository for the collection, and the application of accepted archival standards for storing and making the collection available.

RECORD-KEEPING

Oral history, to be effective and useful, must be documented using procedures that recognize the importance of preservation and accessibility (or usefulness) of the interviews. Three central issues determine the effectiveness of record-keeping. The interview files, whether paper or electronic, must be kept accurately, updated on a timely basis, and maintained in a rational arrangement or order. Interview files include the documents that serve as the interview's formal record. The recordings themselves must be identified clearly so that each recording may be matched to its corresponding interview file. Also, because it is the format most researchers desire, a transcript of each interview (see chapter 6, "Transcribing Oral History") should be prepared and systematically filed for ease of use.

Useful archival interview files begin with well-designed record forms. Typical documents in an interview file include the following: interview checklist, interview summary, and interview release.

Interview Checklist

The *interview checklist* is necessary for internal file control. This form serves as the cover sheet to each interview file and provides a record of the various stages of the interview process from initial contact with the interviewee through archiving of the completed oral history. Typically, an interview checklist is the first page of an interviewee's file and should not be removed from the file folder.

Sections of the interview checklist track all phases of the interview, which vary somewhat from project to project but often include the following: a header containing the project name and affiliation (if applicable); interviewee's full name, address, phone number(s), fax, and e-mail address; interviewer's full name; interview date; interview topics; signed release (verification that the document is signed, dated, and filed); recording duplication and date (whether the recording was duplicated for transcription purposes or to give the interviewee a copy); transcription date or reason why not transcribed (sometimes extremely short or interrupted interviews are not transcribed); transcription information, including the names of transcribers, the date(s) completed, tape number, and number of pages; auditing (whether a person other than the transcriber listened to the recording and verified the

Interview Checklist Elements

- Project name and affiliation
- Interviewee's name and contact information
- Interviewer's name
- Interview date
- Topics
- Signed release (date)
- Duplication date (and number of copies)
- Transcription date (or reason not done)
- Transcription information (transcriber, date, tape number, pages)
- Auditing (review of transcription against tape)
- Editing
- Interviewee review
- Final revisions to the transcript
- Indexing
- List of photographs and supporting documents in file
- Final copy to interviewee (date)
- Duplicate tape to interviewee (date)
- Disposition of original tapes
- Disposition of transcripts
- Disposition of interview files

accuracy of the transcription, including the date); editing (the name of the editor, if different from the transcriber, and the date); interviewee review (if the interviewee is allowed to review the transcription); final revisions to the transcript (following auditing, editing, or interviewee review); indexing (name of indexer and date); list of archival materials or artifacts donated by the interviewee (if these materials are part of the project, there should be a separate release for them); the dates when any final transcriptions or recording duplicates were sent to the interviewee; and disposition of the original tapes, transcripts, and interview files, including location (repository) and date.

Interview Summary

The *interview summary* is a brief narrative description of the interview that covers the major topics related in the course of the interview.

Interview Release

The third form usually found in an interview file is the signed *interview release* (see chapter 4, "Legal Issues," for further information on releases). This form, essential to every oral history project, transfers ownership of the recording to the institution or individual conducting the project. An interview release signed by both interviewee and interviewer at the conclusion of the interview allows researchers, publishers, and audiovisual producers to use the interview. An interview release form must describe the final disposition of the interview and any conditions on its use as a research tool or in final products. Ideally, legal counsel should review this document with attention to copyright law and future potential uses of the interview contents.

An interview file can also contain notes made by the interviewer and other supporting materials relating to the interviewee,

Interview Summary Elements

- Interviewee's name
- Interviewer's name
- Date of interview
- Place of interview
- Length of interview (in minutes)
- Description of interview—a brief summary of topics covered
- Proper spellings of names, places, and any unclear or unfamiliar words

such as copies of photographs, scrapbooks, biographies, and family histories.

Preservation

Preservation of an oral history interview begins prior to or at the scene of the interview with the interviewer's thoughtful selection of recording materials, practices, and setting. The interviewer must properly document the interview recording as soon as it has been created. This means that all documents must be signed and all recordings marked, both physically on the medium and its container and electronically on the recording. If analog tapes are the medium, then mark the tapes and tape cases with the interviewee's and interviewer's names, date, and location of the interview. In the case of digital recordings, the interviewer must document on the recording all of this information and electronically label the recording in a consistent manner when it is downloaded for storage.

Analog or digital recording media should be of sufficient quality for maximum shelf life in an archival storage area or electronic storage platform. Because these media carry the oral histories, this is not the place to save money at the expense of poor quality. The best course of action is to purchase the best media you can afford. Inexpensive materials and lower-quality manufacturing techniques produce media that deteriorate faster. Inexpensive analog tapes are produced on thinner, weaker polyester, to which oxide particles do not adhere as well as they do to thicker, better-made tapes. It is a good idea to buy tapes of at least medium quality or— for a few dollars more—record interviews on top-quality tapes.

Once you complete and turn in the interview, you transfer the responsibility for preservation. Analog tapes are susceptible to physical deterioration due to wear, so repositories routinely make listening (or user) copies and carefully store the originals. Original analog tapes should be protected from dust and stored at temperatures below seventy degrees Fahrenheit and a relative humidity of 40 percent or lower. There are a variety of archival-quality containers available at reasonable prices for storage of physical media of all types. Audiocassettes in archival cassette boxes can be safely stored in microfilm cabinets or in specially designed acid-free archival containers made by a variety of manufacturers and archival suppliers easily found on the Web. Repositories with holdings in analog format must keep and maintain analog playback machines, but conversion of analog recordings to digital format is advisable.

Converting Analog to Digital

Although most oral history projects use digital machines to record interviews, a significant number of programs still use analog tape machines or own previously recorded analog tape recordings. In either case, if analog tapes constitute all or a part of a collection, the recordings should be converted to digital format because analog playback machines are disappearing.

The International Association of Sound and Audiovisual Archives (IASA) recommends the use of an external professional analog/digital (A/D) converter and sound card to perform the conversions. An external A/D converter is necessary because the A/D converters included in typical computer sound cards are not of sufficient quality. Consult the IASA Web site for recommended standards for selecting sampling rate (which fixes the limit on frequency response), bit depth (to capture the full dynamic range of each recording), recording level, target format (PCM .wav files are recommended), and techniques for monitoring the transfer. The interview checklist in the interview file should include a description of how the transfers were conducted: the specifications of any machines used, the technical standards to which the conversion was held, and the monitoring techniques employed.

Once the digital conversion is completed, an uncompressed (digital files lose data when compressed) and unmodified archival .wav file should be preserved electronically (see next section).

Lower-quality user copies can be produced from the master for listening on-site or online.

Preservation of Digital Recordings

Preservation of digital recordings poses special problems; so far, there is no one best solution to preservation given the wide array of projects undertaken and resources available to institutions and individuals conducting oral history projects. Ohio's Digital Resource Commons (DRC), hosted by the Ohio Library and Information Network (OhioLINK), is one institutional repository that enables many institutions (Ohio colleges and universities, in this case) to save and make available online all types of digital formats. Libraries, historical societies, and other institutions host cooperative repositories across the country. There may be no universal solution, but one fact is clear: Archiving electronic recordings will continue to require more digital space.

A related electronic preservation issue is migration of digital audio and video files as systems and formats change. *Migration* is the process of converting old files into new formats. The IASA recommends that recordings be done at the highest quality possible in today's formats to take advantage of the improved formats to come.

The IASA also recommends refraining from editing or making sound improvement (such as noise reduction or equalization) to recordings. Interviews are best archived in their raw, unaltered state; those who work with them in the future can decide how to edit or improve them.

International Association of Sound and Audiovisual Archives (IASA)
http://www.iasa-web.org/index.asp

Collaborative Digitization Program (CDP)
http://www.bcr.org/cdp

Digital Resource Commons (DRC)
http://drc.ohiolink.edu

Because of the uncertainty of digital formats in the future, it is advisable to maintain multiple copies of recordings. Back-up copies stored in different formats will ensure the survival of the recordings for posterity. High-quality read-only optical discs such as CDs and DVDs, magnetic analog data tapes (audiocassettes and videocassettes), and external hard drives are the most practical and economically viable alternatives. There are acid-free archival containers specially designed to safely store optical discs just as there are containers for traditional magnetic tapes.

Although currently unavailable to many institutions and individuals, an institutional network of interconnected hard drives (also called a *redundant array of independent drives*—RAID) or a large institutional server (called a *digital mass storage system*—DMSS) can be a higher-end preservation solution for oral history recordings. Server storage can be configured to back up data, check system integrity, and migrate from old to new systems with relative ease. Regardless of the method of electronic or physical storage, the repository staff should regularly monitor the storage environment and condition of the recordings.

Researchers typically want to read transcriptions instead of reviewing videos. Although transcribing is discussed in chapter 6, there are a few points to be made here regarding preservation and access. Transcriptions should be printed on acid-free paper, placed into acid-free folders, and stored in acid-free boxes available from archival supply companies. Like the recordings themselves, you can store electronic transcriptions effectively on back-up systems, servers, or hard drives. Place printed transcriptions in interview files, which are generally arranged alphabetically by interviewees' surnames.

In the archival setting, researchers locate and assess the appropriateness of a collection for their research by inspecting a variety of *finding aids* that provide information about a collection through a narrative description and a list of files or containers. Oral history collections are typically filed alphabetically, but a finding aid may be arranged by topic (especially in the case of online finding aids, which sometimes are accessed through library online catalogs). Another type of finding aid that was in use even before computers came onto the scene is the *index*. Oral history recordings are often indexed by counter number or by elapsed time (in minutes and seconds) so researchers who want to listen to or view a recording may search for particular parts of the interview. The archival standards section later in this chapter says more about finding aids.

Duplication and copyright of transcripts are also dealt with in chapters 4 and 6, but these issues are linked to accessibility and future use by users and are therefore important considerations in archiving oral history.

SELECTING A REPOSITORY

Maximize long-term sustainability of a collection of interviews by carefully selecting a repository where preservation and accessibility are ensured. Some oral history projects are so product driven—that is, focused on a particular exhibit, documentary, or book—that it becomes easy to overlook the long-term research value of the interviews. Even in the case of a short, simple project that perhaps consists of only four interviews, the information collected from interviewees usually provides raw data that will interest a future researcher. A small collection may represent one topic in a larger local or regional collection and may be very useful when placed in context with the larger collection by an archivist's well-written description and arrangement. A small collection of interviews can be placed in a repository that will preserve it and make it accessible even after the initial product (book, film, radio program) has been completed.

The most logical repository is often one in the immediate geographical area where the interviewees experienced the events related in the interviews. If there is a local library or archives nearby, make an appointment to speak with archival staff. If there is no obvious local choice, an Internet search can help narrow the number of options prior to visiting prospective repositories. Most repositories include their collection development policies online along with collection-level descriptions and inventories. The quality of finding aids online

An interviewee shows photographs and other historical documents to an interviewer. Oral history projects and archives need to develop clear guidelines for the public presentation and storage of these materials. *Courtesy of the Rural Life Center, Kenyon College*

can assist in choosing the right repository for a collection. Pay attention to the repository's hours, availability to the public and scholars, and the staff's professional credentials. Visiting the institution will also provide visible clues about attitudes toward preservation of and access to collections. If collections are haphazardly stored, roughly handled, or difficult to find, consider a different repository.

It is important not only to assess the quality of collections management (storage, preservation, finding aids, and handling policies) but also to understand the types and typical details of agreements each repository favors. Most repositories are not interested in donations carrying severe restrictions on use (except in the case of an exceedingly valuable collection), but negotiations with the head of the department should include potential restrictions you wish to attach to a collection. Remember, archives and special collections departments want not only to preserve collections but also to make them accessible to people seeking information.

Oral History Association (OHA) http://alpha.dickinson.edu/oha

The Society of American Archivists (SAA) http://www.archivists.org

The Society of American Archivists (SAA) and the Oral History Association (OHA) are two professional organizations that provide standards, guidelines, and best practices for oral history collections. Information regarding oral history archiving is available on the Web sites of both organizations. Since most repositories list their policies online, you can compare these posted policies to see if they are compatible with OHA and SAA standards.

Basic archival standards developed by the SAA and OHA provide a baseline for archiving oral history projects. Once a repository accepts materials from an oral history project, it assumes responsibility for proper storage, preservation, preparation of useful finding aids, publicity announcing the existence of the collection, availability of the collection in that particular repository, and ethical handling of and access to the collection.

Archivists refer to storage as one of the elements of *physical control* of a collection. Structurally sound shelving and acid-free, lignin-free containers are essential to effective storage. Tapes, files, photographs, and other media can damage each other through reactions among their chemical substrates; even collections stored all together in one place (not always the case in an archive) should be stored in different containers.

Another facet of safe storage, particularly of such unique materials as oral histories, is the maintenance of closed stacks. That is, patrons are not allowed into the storage areas; staff or volunteers retrieve archival materials and bring them to the patron in a controlled reading room. Patrons are supervised as they access materials, which assures that files are not intermingled between folders or folders between boxes. This level of records control decreases the chance of losing or misfiling materials.

There are two other elements of preservation in archival work. A repository should be able to maintain average temperature and relative humidity levels within the optimum ranges of fifty-five to sixty-five degrees Fahrenheit (thirteen to eighteen degrees Celsius) and 30 to 40 percent relative humidity for most archival materials. Also, responsible repositories have certain handling policies for staff as well as patrons. For example, staff and patrons should handle photographic prints and negatives with clean cotton gloves. Since excessive handling damages collections, it is a fairly common policy to allow only staff members to photocopy materials for patrons. Typically, modern archives charge more than the local photocopy store in order to recover overhead costs like staff time.

Prospective oral history collection users primarily locate materials of interest through finding aids the archival staff prepares. Archivists refer to these hierarchical documents as *intellectual control*—different levels of description depending on the complexity of each collection. The simplest finding aid is a collection-level description. Patrons may access this type of finding aid through the National Union Catalog of Manuscript Collections (NUCMC), which is available online, and through library online catalogs. Finding aids available on the Internet provide the widest possible user base for collections, so to maximize accessibility, it is advisable to house collections in repositories with online capabilities.

Another recent development is the advent of scanned or otherwise electronically viewable transcriptions. However, oral history projects planning to put transcripts online should inform interviewees of the worldwide public accessibility of their testimony.

Archives and other types of repositories must always consider ethical issues as well. All previous restrictions agreed to must be honored, so personal information must be withheld from researchers if specified by an agreement. Personal information in a collection cannot be accessible to any users. Also, all agreements regarding use must be in the files, or materials may not be viewed by patrons. It is a repository's responsibility

National Union Catalog of Manuscript Collections (NUCMC) http://www.loc.gov/coll/nucmc

to keep accurate records and make materials accessible but protect the interviewees who provided the information.

The archival integrity of an oral history collection begins in the planning stage before any interviews are conducted. The advisory committee, project coordinator, interviewers, transcribers, and production people all play a role in archiving just as the archivist does once an oral history collection reaches a repository. Archiving an oral history properly is a commitment not only to future researchers who will use it, but also to the interviewee who donated his or her memories.

NOTES

1. Stephen H. Paschen, *Shootin' the Chutes: Amusement Parks Remembered* (Akron, Ohio: Summit County Historical Society, 1988).

Chapter Ten

Funding

By Donna M. DeBlasio and David H. Mould

Raising money for an oral history project? It's not nearly as exciting as planning the project, doing the interviews, and sharing them with audiences. However, unless you have a professional fund-raiser on staff, it's a task you'll need to take on. Approach it with the same energy and passion that you bring to every other aspect of the project. You need to be able to explain what you want to do and why it's important to a funder who has many other requests. Why is your project more deserving than a summer soccer camp for children, a university lecture series, or a traditional music festival? And how will support for your project enhance the funder's public image? Asking for money not only helps you figure out what a project is really going to cost but also makes you answer the key planning question: Who cares? Your goal is to convince people that your project will make the world (or, at least, your little corner of it) a better place—and then to pay for it.

DO YOU NEED TO WRITE A GRANT PROPOSAL?

If you can skip the paperwork and go straight to a funding source, do so. If you have a small project and need only a few hundred dollars, writing a grant may not be worth the effort. Do what every school or community organization does: Ask for contributions from local businesses, such as banks, realtors, lawyers, and insurance agencies, and community and professional clubs and organizations. Maybe other people involved in the project can each pledge to sign up two or three local sponsors. Maybe the mayor's office has a discretionary fund for small projects. Appeal to community spirit—with some subtle prodding: "I just received $100 from the law firm of Dolittle and Dally. They mentioned that your company was a client and suggested I contact you."

This approach may work when a funder sees direct benefits. It's not too difficult to persuade a university alumni association that it's a good idea to interview the class of 1939 or to sell the idea of a documentary on the life-and-death experiences of firefighters to the city council. The potential problem comes with taking money from an organization that may want to dictate how the history is collected, edited, and presented. When oral historians Michael and Carrie Nobel Kline accepted a contract to do an oral history of the U.S. Army Corps of Engineers Huntingdon District, they were assured they would have freedom to talk to current and former Corps staffers and to explore all sides of the story, including congressional lobbying and community opposition to projects. Two years and more than sixty interviews later, just as their oral history was about to go to press, the Corps killed the project and told them to return the tapes. Did the Corps lose interest or have fears about the agency's public image? Michael and Carrie may never know because the Corps claims their interviews are works made for hire and cannot be published without permission. They had worked hard to present a balanced history and cited the achievements of the Corps while giving voice to those who were angry that dams displace people. Doing oral history on a contract basis for a corporation, agency, or organization assures funding but has ethical pitfalls.

In most cases, you will need to write a grant proposal. An excellent free source of advice is the Grantsmanship Center, which provides a state-by-state listing of foundations and corporate giving programs and links to state government Web sites where grants and bids are announced; links to federal government grants on the *Federal Register* (which is much easier than trying to navigate the *Federal Register* itself); and some international sources. There's a useful listing of Web resources for funding organizations from the W. K. Kellogg Foundation. (Go to Grantseeking and Grantseeking Tips.) These include the Foundation Center, which claims to maintain a comprehensive database on U.S. grantmakers and their grants. Some larger organizations seeking major grants subscribe to the Foundation Directory online. Several universities offer publicly available grant-finding aids—one of the best is from Michigan State University library. It lists grants for nonprofits by subject categories; grants for individuals; and links to federal funding sources, national, and international funders.

Proposals come in all shapes, sizes, and lengths—from the short online proposal for corporate and community foundations to the lengthy annotated proposals that major agencies

General Guidelines for Finding Funding

1. Do your homework.
2. Complete the application the way the funder wants it completed.
3. Learn the lingo.
4. Be neat and accurate.
5. Submit a preliminary proposal.
6. Be accountable—to your funder, organization, and audience. Do what you say you're going to do.
7. Don't promise more than you can deliver for the budget granted.

require. One filmmaker colleague compared writing a National Endowment for the Humanities proposal to writing a master's thesis. He was only half joking. In general, the more money you're asking for, the longer the proposal. Let's begin by reviewing the types of sponsors you could approach for funding.

State Humanities Councils

State humanities councils (the name varies, but every U.S. state has one) are the most reliable and predictable source of oral history funding. The program officers and grant reviewers know what oral history is, so you don't need to craft a literature review or make an argument as to why oral history is needed to balance other historical accounts. However, because humanities councils often support oral history projects, they receive many grant applications. You need to show, for example, that you're not simply interviewing all the World War II veterans or retired steelworkers because they're getting older every year and no one has recorded their memories. This is a project without a clear purpose, or *salvage folklore*. Instead, you need to show what the interviews will add to the historical record, what they can tell us about changing attitudes toward war and conflict or the social and economic impact of manufacturing, and how the project will engage new audiences in exploring their history. Humanities councils rarely fund oral history projects that do not include some type of public program in which the interviews are shared with audiences. They are generally open to various presentation formats, including museum and library exhibitions, theatrical presentations, audio and video documentaries, multimedia presentations, and Web sites (or some combination of formats). Because of their relatively high costs, video documentaries are likely to receive the most budget scrutiny. You need to justify the choice of video by showing that this is the most effective medium to reach the largest audience. If you could reach the same audience with an exhibit at the city library, then maybe that's what you should be doing.

What Goes into a Grant Application?

1. Description of the organization, including its mission
2. Qualifications of key personnel
3. Budget summary
4. What the organization will do with the money and why
5. Publicity
6. Assessment tools

Humanities scholars must be closely involved. That means academics with PhDs in the humanities, which (according to Congress) include archaeology; comparative religion; ethics; history; languages and linguistics; literature; jurisprudence; philosophy; the history, theory, and criticism of the arts; and aspects of the social sciences that use historical or philosophical approaches. This can seem like an unnecessary burden. After all, you're the local expert. You know the history of your community better than some associate professor who's never even visited your town. However, that's not the point. The role of a humanities scholar is to connect your oral history project to broader themes and trends in history—in sum, to help you to make the stories of war veterans or retired steelworkers relevant beyond your community. The scholars can also help you avoid factual mistakes and suggest how to organize and present your materials. Because they are usually not from your community, they can take a more dispassionate and critical view of the oral history. You can certainly ask them to work pro bono, but most humanities councils will be happier if you offer a modest honorarium.

State Arts Councils

State arts councils, by contrast, usually want you to pay the artists, not the scholars. Because arts councils fund many kinds of art (visual art, textiles, dance, music) and activities (exhibitions, concerts, performances, school programs), it's more difficult to find a fit for an oral history project. The words to look for in the proposal guidelines are *documentation* and *preservation.* If you're planning to interview sculptors, classical composers, quilters, or old-time banjo players or to document the artistic expressions of ethnic communities, then an arts council may fund your project. Many councils have separate grant deadlines and review panels for different areas of the arts. It's worth checking funding history—the types of projects the panel has funded in the last three to five years. There's no point in taking your old-time banjo project to the music panel if it funds only concerts, performances, and education programs or only projects on classical music; the traditional and ethnic arts panel (which may actually include one or two old-time banjo players) is a surer bet.

Federal, State, and Local Government Authorities

Many people outside government (and some inside it) are surprised to learn that federal and state agencies have historians on the staff, employ contract historians, and sometimes accept bids or grant proposals for oral history projects. The federal government has a long history of funding oral history projects. In 1935, Congress established the Works Progress Administration (WPA) to provide work for unemployed Americans. Under the WPA Federal Writers' Project, historians and writers collected interviews with former slaves; more than two thousand men and women were interviewed between 1936 and 1938 for what became known as the WPA Slave Narratives. All branches of the military, federal agencies, and both houses of Congress conduct historical research, not only on their own institutional past but also on a range of social, economic, and cultural issues. Since 2001, the U.S. Department of Education has funded a program called Teaching American History to expand the knowledge of K–12 teachers.

At the state and local levels, historical research has become an essential part of planning decisions. Any new highway, urban redevelopment, or zoning regulation has a potential historical as well as an environmental impact. Although most research focuses on the preservation of historic buildings and sites, oral history is often useful—for example, to document changes in land use and settlement or developments in agriculture. Most such projects employ a range of historical methods with an emphasis on document and legal research, but oral history can fill gaps in the record. At the local level, think about how urban and community development projects can incorporate oral history. For example, the city runs a summer education and sports program for teens. Why not suggest training small groups of teens in interviewing, video recording, and editing and have them undertake a project? Or perhaps there's money for sprucing up the historical district. Why not add an oral history project in which older residents recall how the neighborhood has changed? The key is to find a larger, more generic project and to show what oral history can add to it.

Foundations and Private Sources

Hundreds of foundations across the country offer funding for community development, education, public health, the arts and culture, and many other social causes. Broadly speaking, there are three types of foundations—private, community, and corporate. Private foundations, such as the W. K. Kellogg Foundation and the Annie E. Casey Foundation, support civic education, community development, and media and have funded many oral history projects. Some private foundations invest only in projects that are national in scope and have the potential to reach a large audience. If you think your project fits a foundation's guidelines, the next step is to check funding history—the types of projects funded and the grant amounts.

Community Foundations. Almost every city large enough to have elected officials, a telephone directory, and a strip mall has a community foundation that sponsors programs within a specific

Documenting Your Project

1. How you spent your grant money
2. How you assessed your project
3. Photos or video if appropriate to your project
4. Examples of publicity (newspaper articles, audio and/or video clips, flyers, invitations)

geographic area. The foundation raises money from individuals and businesses in the community and spends it in and on the community. In metropolitan areas, city foundations have an office, a full-time staff and a blue-ribbon board of directors that includes prominent business people, lawyers, elected officials, artists, and philanthropists; they hand out hundreds of thousands of dollars a year to major arts and culture organizations, universities, schools, and hospitals. In smaller cities, the foundation has a similar professional mix but no office or staff and a much smaller budget; it may hand out a couple of $10,000 grants, but most will be under $5,000.

The first and most important rule is that you need to be local and have a local project. Community foundations do not fund projects outside the city limits or even in the suburbs. Because they review and fund many kinds of projects, their grant proposal guidelines tend to be broad. Remember that your proposal is not in competition with other oral history projects (as with state humanities councils) but with a wide range of social, educational, and artistic projects. You need to convince the foundation that what you're proposing is a better investment than playground equipment or a chamber music series. The comparison may seem harsh, but realistically these are the hard choices that community foundations have to make.

Corporate Foundations. The most useful guides to corporate foundations are not only in books or Web sites. If you want to know where funding is available, look at a map of retail locations or utility service areas. Some retail chains fund projects only in areas where they have stores. The Kroger Company Foundation supports charitable activities in the communities where Kroger customers and associates live and work. The Safeway Foundation focuses its funding in eighteen states, mostly in the Great Plains, Mountain West area, West Coast, Maryland, Virginia, and Washington, DC. There are Wal-Mart stores in all fifty states, but the Wal-Mart Foundation gives more money in its home state of Arkansas than anywhere else. And if you're looking for a grant from the Dollar General Foundation, you need to live within twenty miles of a store in the company's thirty-five-state market area. The same goes for utilities, including electricity, gas, and telephone companies. The American Electric Power (AEP) Foundation will consider projects outside its eleven-state service area; however, a proposal from California will stand less chance of getting funding than one from a state where AEP has a regional utility company. Both the AT&T Foundation and the Verizon Foundation fund only in communities where they provide home telephone service. This can become a tricky mapping exercise, especially in rural areas where communities a few miles apart have different phone providers. Cell phone coverage doesn't count—you can have a strong AT&T cell phone signal, but if you're in the Verizon area, you can't get a grant from AT&T. However, some corporate foundations have no geographic restrictions.

Why would a corporate foundation consider funding an oral history project? It's all part of corporate social responsibility, an attractive-sounding if ill-defined concept. Corporations that make money in communities need to show they're good corporate citizens helping to make the communities better places to live and work. Education and health are the top priorities for most corporate foundations, but funding goals are broadly defined. The AT&T Foundation focuses on education initiatives from reducing high school dropout rates to preparing young people to enter the workforce. There's no mention of oral history, but a schools-based project with measurable educational outcomes might qualify. Among the Kroger Company Foundation's priorities are breast cancer initiatives and disaster relief. What about oral history projects with breast cancer survivors and disaster victims? You will need to make the case that oral history can serve a therapeutic or educational need, but there's research to support this. Focus areas for the AEP Foundation include education, health, and the environment. Energy companies, always keen to improve their public image, need to show they are friends of the environment, and that could include funding an oral history project. AEP could also fund an oral history project through its focus on art, music, and cultural heritage in communities. It's unlikely a corporate foundation will support an oral history project that results only in new research but no public programs. However, a project that brings together schools, community organizations, and local government, offers public programs, and attracts media coverage will be more appealing.

Historical Organizations

What about pitching your project to your local or state historical society? You'll likely receive advice and encouragement but no money. That's because historical organizations are often short of resources and are themselves seeking grants for new projects. However, some city or county historical societies are supported by local benefactors or receive large estate gifts, so it's always worth asking. One supporter of local history projects has been the History Channel, which launched its Save Our History grants program in 2004. The purpose is to "inspire the youth in your community to become the preservationists of tomorrow." Local historical societies, museums, historic sites, preservation organizations, libraries, and archives are encouraged to partner with schools or youth groups to preserve local history. The grants (maximum $10,000) are awarded once a year. In 2007–8, more than half the projects funded included the collecting of oral histories.

HOW TO RESEARCH AND APPROACH A FUNDING SOURCE

The first step is to research the funder, its history, mission, and priorities. Information will be available from the funder's Web site and from the online sources on foundations and funding agencies. Funding priorities are sometimes frustratingly vague;

What Makes a Grant-Funded Project Successful?

1. The grant was well written.
2. The project was appropriate to the organization and to the qualifications of the staff.
3. There were other sources of support whether in-kind or monetary.
4. There was a well-developed publicity plan.
5. Performances and presentations were free and open to the general public.
6. The organization followed proper procedures in closing out the grant.
7. The project made a lasting contribution to the community.

almost every corporate foundation claims it wants to improve the quality of life in the communities where it does business. The best guide to whether your project is a fit is to study funding history. Many funders publish lists of organizations and projects funded; some give brief descriptions of the projects. Funding history is also a good indication of how much money to request. Most funders will provide a top limit, but that's usually not representative of the typical amount awarded. Consider calling or e-mailing an organization that received funding to ask about its experience, and ask to read its winning proposal.

Many funders provide grant applications, guidelines, and answers to frequently asked questions on their Web sites. In some cases, you need to submit a letter of inquiry, a letter of intent, or a short prospectus before submitting a full application. In other cases, you can submit an application without a preliminary review. Some funders now accept only online grant applications.

State humanities councils welcome phone and e-mail inquiries from applicants. The program officers do not make funding decisions but will help you craft a proposal that addresses the criteria, provide the names of humanities scholars who can serve as advisors, and make sure your budget looks reasonable.

It's their job to answer questions and make sure that the proposals that come to the review panel are clear and focused. If your proposal is rejected, they can help you decide whether it's worth rewriting and resubmitting for the next funding round.

Program officers from federal and state government agencies are also available to answer questions, although sometimes the scope of inquiry may be limited. Corporate and private foundations are less responsive partly because the foundation officers are often also the decision-makers and need to avoid a conflict of interest. Some private foundations do not accept unsolicited proposals. Instead, they actively seek projects in their areas of interest and then encourage proposals. Some program officers will talk to you and give advice; others prohibit all contact.

Questions to Ask before You Submit a Proposal

Does my organization have the capacity to take on this project? This is a planning question that you—and your staff or board—need to consider before putting effort into a grant proposal. If you receive the grant, will you have the people, facilities, and time to undertake the project and stay within the budget? If the answer is maybe or don't know, then perhaps it's time to stop, take a deep breath, and figure out whether to bring in a partner organization, reduce the scope of the project, or drop the idea altogether. Too many small organizations take on ambitious projects with inadequate resources and funding and run into trouble.

Does my organization qualify for a grant? Most corporate and private foundations accept applications only from 501(c)(3) organizations that have been granted nonprofit, tax-exempt classification under the Internal Revenue Code. That's because of the tax benefits: The grant will be counted as a charitable contribution. However, not all 501(c)(3) organizations may be eligible. Some funders will not give grants to religious and political organizations, advocacy groups, or charities that distribute aid outside the United States. And not all tax-exempt organizations are 501(c)(3) groups; a state university, for example, is tax-exempt but not under 501(c)(3). Federal and state funding agencies provide a list of the types of qualifying organizations in their requests for applications. State humanities and arts councils have the most flexible guidelines; generally, an organization needs to be nonprofit in intent but may not have applied for 501(c)(3) status.

What should go into a letter of intent (LOI) or a preproposal? There are two types of letters of intent. One simply notifies the funder that you plan to submit a proposal. It should be concise and clear, but the content will not be considered in the funding decision. The second type is essentially a preproposal; it will be used to decide whether to invite you to submit a full proposal. The LOI should contain a brief description of your project and its significance *and clearly relate it to the funder's mission and priorities;* background on your organization, experience, and capacity to undertake the project; a list of partners or organizations that support the project; and a cost estimate that includes what you have raised (or plan to raise) from other sources and resources you will contribute.

Common Proposal Areas and Questions

Follow the Grant Guidelines. Assuming there's a decent fit between your project and the funder's priorities, make sure that you closely follow the guidelines. This means responding to every question on an application, even if it does not seem to apply to your project. Some applicants find it easy to write at length (and with enthusiasm) about the history of their communities but give less space and attention to how they plan to document this history. If you've got a five-page narrative limit and spend four pages sketching out the historical background, start over—make the narrative more concise. Remember that you're not asking for funding for history itself but for its documentation. If the funder lists criteria it will use to assess the proposal, make sure you address them. Federal and state agencies have specific requirements for paper and online applications that include the filing of compliance and disclosure forms, budget templates, appendices, curriculum vitae, and other items. Make sure you follow these closely, or your proposal may be rejected on technical grounds because it does not meet the standard submission requirements.

Summary of Project. You will likely have to provide a three-hundred- to five-hundred-word summary or abstract of the project. It's often best to write this after you've drafted the rest of the proposal. It should capture the essence and significance of the project by relating it to the funder's priorities, describing how the project will be distributed and who will benefit from it. Don't oversell your project with terms such as *unique, state of the art,* or *highly acclaimed.* Adjectival fluff irritates reviewers. Use the limited number of words available to make sure that the reader has a clear understanding of what you plan to do.

Statement of Need/Significance of Project. You need to make the case for why the funder should support this project. What will the interviews contribute to understanding of the history of a community, industry, or ethnic group? Why has this topic been neglected? Is this a one-off project or part of a larger and longer effort? Who will benefit directly or indirectly?

Advisors. Some funders want community members to be involved in planning and guiding the project. Even if this is not required, it's often worth forming a project advisory board. For a humanities project, humanities scholars must be directly involved in conceptualization and execution. If you're doing a museum exhibit, a radio series, a video documentary, or an interactive Web site, you will need technical advisors.

Organization Description. What are the mission and history of your organization? Describe other historical and oral history projects it has undertaken, such as public programs, exhibitions, and media as well as their audiences and results. If your organization is not clearly involved in history, you need to show how oral history fits its mission. Do you have enough staff members or volunteers to undertake this project? Have other people or organizations in your community volunteered to help? Who will manage the accounts and provide reports to the funder?

Project Planning and Activities. How much planning has already been done, and what remains to be done? List the stages of the project as specifically as possible—for example, the number of interviews planned and how interviewees will be selected; how interviewers will be selected, trained, and supervised; how the interviews will be transcribed and processed; and how the oral history will be presented and archived.

Audience. Most funders (and definitely humanities and arts councils) want public programs that reach the largest, most diverse audiences possible. You will need to describe the forums and media in which oral history will be shared and how you will advertise and market the programs. Although the interviews may end up in an archive and be made available to researchers, research projects are generally less attractive to funders than are those that reach a general (nonacademic) audience.

Goals, Objectives, and Evaluation. Funders like things they can measure, count, and then feature in press releases, annual reports, and Web sites. Although your project goals may be broad—to raise community historical consciousness, for example, or to engage young people in history—grant reviewers look for more tangible outcomes. Some can be pretty straightforward—the number of interviews collected, the number of people attending a public program, the number of Web site hits, or a list of articles about the project. You should also plan to collect ratings and comments from people who attend a program and suggestions for future projects.

Accuracy and Clarity. It's always good to have other people read and critique the proposal. Something that may have seemed very clear to you when you wrote it may puzzle or confuse them. If that's the case, rewrite the unclear section(s). Make sure the narrative is free of grammar and spelling errors and that the budget numbers add up.

DOING THE BUDGET

This is often the most challenging part of a proposal. There's always a temptation to underbudget a project in the hope this will improve your chances of getting the grant. That's usually a mistake. Funding agencies regularly review proposals and have a good idea of how much things cost. An unrealistic budget may raise questions about other parts of the proposal or your ability to complete the project. We do not recommend padding budgets but suggest you use realistic figures for salaries, benefits, travel, and supplies. Because of funding restrictions, your organization may need to pay for some items; a funder may not allow you to purchase equipment such as camcorders, computers, or printers but will pay for tapes, discs, and office supplies, and staff to shoot and transcribe interviews. Many projects are funded from several grants; indeed, funders like to see that a project has support from several sources. Once you've secured a grant, you can use it to show *cost share* in another grant proposal. There are some restrictions; for example, you can't use federal funds as a match for federal funds. But you can match federal against state dollars (or vice versa) and use private dollars as a match in federal or state grants.

There are two kinds of costs. *Direct* (or above-the-line) costs refer to what you need to accomplish a specific project: staff salaries, benefits, supplies, travel, transcribing, marketing, printing. *Indirect* (or below-the-line) costs refer to the ongoing expenses of your organization: staff salaries, benefits, rent, utilities, telephone, insurance, computers. Although *indirect* costs (also called *overhead*) are not directly attributable to the project, they need to be included to estimate the true cost; if you didn't have an office with computers and a phone, you could not undertake the project. Many organizations use a percentage of a total project budget to calculate indirect costs. Most federal and state funding agencies allow indirect costs with rates varying from 10 to 50 percent depending on the type of project. Large private foundations may allow indirect costs; many corporate and community foundations and state humanities and arts councils prohibit them. If that's the case, you may be able to include indirect costs (what you would have charged if you had been allowed to do so) as part of your *in-kind match*. This needs to be distinguished from your *cost share*—the cash you'll be contributing from another grant, ticket sales, or concessions. The *in-kind match* is your organization's noncash contribution to the project; it can include staff time, space, facilities, and equipment. For example, if the local library lets you use a room free of charge for your public program or exhibit, you can count the normal rental cost of the room as in-kind. If the public radio station lets you borrow audio recording equipment and edit interviews, you can count the cost of the equipment and editing facility rental. Some grant application guidelines list categories that can be counted as in-kind, but if you're in doubt call the program officer.

We suggest you develop a template with categories that you use for every proposal. It will need to be adapted because each funder wants the budget presented in a specific way or on a specific form, but keeping a list of categories will ensure that you don't overlook something.

Sample Budget

Budget item	Item cost	Grant request	Cost share: foundation	Cost share: revenue	In-kind
Project director salary, 10 days @ $300 per day	$3,000	$2,000			$1,000
Project director benefits	$750	$500			$250
Audio editor/technician	$1,500	$1,500			
Two volunteer interviewers, 10 days @ $200 per day	$2,000				$2,000
Interview travel and meal expenses for volunteers	$2,000	$1,000	$1,000		
Interview transcription, 140 hours @ $20 per hour	$2,800	$2,800			
Honoraria for two humanities scholars @ $350	$700	$700			
Honorarium for evaluator	$350	$350			
Honoraria for six musicians @ $250	$1,500		$1,000	$500	
Travel and meals for scholars and evaluator	$400	$400			
Rental of audio equipment	$1,000		$250		$750
Rental of editing equipment	$1,000		$250		$750
Audio tapes	$250	$250			
Office supplies	$100	$100			
Photocopies	$100		$100		
Publicity and marketing	$500	$250	$250		
Community center for public presentation	$250				$250
Performance space	$300	$150	$150		
Rental of sound equipment for performance	$500			$500	
Indirect costs (10 percent of grant)	$1,000				$1,000
Total	**$20,000**	**$10,000**	**$3,000**	**$1,000**	**$6,000**

Here's a sample budget for an oral history project on local traditional musicians with five short radio features, a public presentation and discussion, and a performance by the musicians. The total budget is $20,000. You're asking the state humanities council for $10,000 and need to provide a 1:1 match. You've already received a $3,000 grant from a community foundation (*cost share: foundation*), and you expect to make $1,000 from ticket sales and concessions at the concert (*cost share: revenue*). You need to show another $6,000 in in-kind match. Note that several items—for example, the project director's salary and benefits, interview travel and meal expenses, publicity and marketing—are budgeted from more than one source.

STAY IN TOUCH

Funders always like to know how a project is going. Some require regular (quarterly or biannual) reports and accounts; for others, only a final report and budget may be needed. Whatever the rules, you'll stay on the funder's good side if you provide regular short updates. Program officers need to track the progress of projects so they can make presentations to the board of directors, answer questions, write annual reports, and update their Web sites. Keeping them informed with a short e-mail report and a couple of photos, a link to a news article on the project, or some press clippings will mean that they remember your project. This takes time, but staying in touch will help position your organization to go back to the funder for that next oral history project.

Chapter Eleven

Sharing Oral History

By Donna M. DeBlasio

You've collected oral history interviews. Now what will you do with them? Since oral history's inception, researchers and others have used these histories in a multitude of ways. They were originally used mainly by people researching material for publication. Scholars in particular have long treated oral histories as primary sources, although there is still some controversy over their value as historical evidence. While publications are the most obvious outlet for oral histories, in recent years interviews have gone beyond the print medium. Technologies old and new make use of oral history interviews in exciting and novel ways. In some cases, the interviews were used in ways never intended by their creators. In others, the interviews were collected for a specific purpose. No matter how they are used, making oral history accessible to as many people as possible in any media is as important as collecting the interviews themselves.

PUBLICATIONS

Studs Terkel, Chicago broadcaster turned historian, was one of the first to use oral history in popular publications. Beginning with *Hard Times: An Oral History of the Great Depression* in 1970, Terkel used interviews, many with ordinary people, to tell the story of one of the most traumatic eras in American (and world) history. He followed *Hard Times* with other oral history-based works that include the highly acclaimed *Working: People Talk About What They Do All Day and How They Feel About What They Do* (1974) and the Pulitzer Prize–winning *The Good War: An Oral History of World War II* (1985), which painted a complex picture of World War II and the people who lived through it. Terkel's publications were enormously successful, reached a very broad audience, publicized oral history, and encouraged many to begin collecting their own interviews.

Terkel's works are among the best known that use oral history, at least to the general public. Many others have made judicious use of oral history interviews, including publications that pair words with photographs. One such recent work is *The Italian American Experience in New Haven: Images and Oral Histories* by Anthony V. Riccio (2006). This lavish coffee-table book, while meant for popular consumption, is grounded in scholarship and provides an insightful and fascinating look into the everyday lives of the members of this immigrant community. By juxtaposing images of the interviewees and their families, neighborhoods, and other local landmarks with the interviews, the reader can really gain an understanding of and appreciation for New Haven's Italian Americans.

Scholars in various fields have also made excellent use of oral histories that often challenge existing notions of personalities and events. One of oral history's most important uses has been to illuminate the lives of people who do not fit into traditional histories. The working class, for example, has only recently become widely studied. In works such as *Like a Family: The Making of a Southern Cotton Mill World* by Jacquelyn Dowd Hall, *The Face of Decline: The Pennsylvania Anthracite Coal Mining Region in the Twentieth Century* by Thomas Dublin and Walter Licht, and *Black Workers Remember: An Oral History of*

Segregation, Unionism, and the Freedom Struggle by Michael Honey, oral histories play a key role in interpreting the lives of the working class and greatly expanding the knowledge of the field of labor history. Steven High uses oral histories to help document the story of deindustrialization and its impact on rust belt communities in North America in *Industrial Sunset: The Making of North America's Rust Belt, 1969–1984*. Native Americans, many of whom transmitted their past through the oral tradition, have also been the subjects of recent publications that use oral history interviews. *Nations Remembered: An Oral History of the Five Civilized Tribes, 1865–1907* by Theda Perdu is just one example of a scholarly work dealing with Native American history. Women's history has greatly benefited from the use of oral history interviews as primary sources. A sample of these works includes *Homesteading Women: An Oral History of Colorado, 1890–1950* by Julie Jones-Eddy, *Rosie the Riveter Revisited: Women, the War, and Social Change* by Sherna Berger Gluck, and *Work, Family, and Faith: Rural Southern Women in the Twentieth Century* edited by Melissa Walker and Rebecca Sharpless.

Oral history has also enriched the story of men and women during wartime, whether in the military or in civilian life. The interviews in Al Santoli's *Everything We Had: An Oral History of the Vietnam War* put a human face on America's longest and one of its most divisive wars. He interviewed not only soldiers but also nurses, medics, CIA operatives, and others. Knowledge about World War II, always a topic of great interest, has certainly been gained from a wide range of interviews, many of which have appeared in numerous scholarly and popular publications. *Bloods: An Oral History of the Vietnam War by Black Veterans* by Wallace Terry provides an insightful and stunning perspective on Vietnam as well. One unusual publication dealing with World War II is *GI Jews: How World War II Changed a Generation* by Deborah Dash Moore. The author chronicles the lives of fifteen Jewish men as they deal with being a part of the U.S. armed forces; oral histories provide important primary source materials for this work.

Authors have also examined areas of history that may not seem quite as weighty as wars or labor conflicts but that tell us something about our lives. Leisure-time activities may seem like a somewhat frivolous topic for historical inquiry, but how we play tells us as much about ourselves as how we work. Oral histories provide fine sources of information to study this aspect of our culture. For example, a recent book by Lu Vickers and Sara Dionne documented the history of one of the nation's kitschiest attractions, the mermaids of Weeki Wachee in Florida. In *Weeki Wachee, City of Mermaids: A History of One of Florida's Oldest Roadside Attractions,* the authors used oral histories to document the story of one venue for American leisure culture. Amusement parks are another form of leisure activity whose history has been chronicled in oral interviews. For example, Carrie Knight used interviews to explore the history of the carousel, an amusement park staple, in *The Carousel Keepers: An Oral History of American Carousels.* Popular music has also provided oral history fodder. Alan Lysaght and David Pritchard provide insight into a worldwide cultural phenomenon in *The Beatles: An Oral History.*

Some publications using oral history have not only challenged the dead great white man's version of the past but have also forced us to rethink our concepts of how people remember the past. Alessandro Portelli's essay, "The Death of Luigi Trastulli," is the seminal work in demonstrating how people remember traumatic events. Trastulli was a steelworker in the staunchly leftist city of Terni, about sixty miles north of Rome, Italy. He was killed during an anti-NATO rally in 1949. In conducting his interviews, Portelli discovered that Trastulli's death carried meaning and significance far beyond the incident itself: "Its importance lies, rather, in the fact that it became the ground upon which collective memory and imagination built a cluster of tales, symbols, legends and imaginary reconstructions." In fact, the most common error was confusing the place and date of Trastulli's untimely demise.[1] Most of the interviewees claimed he was killed during street fighting that occurred over the mass layoffs at the steel mill in 1953 instead of being killed in anti-NATO riots. Portelli raised important questions regarding use of oral history and the meaning of subjectivity in using interviews as research tools. The oral historian needs to be aware that people do not remember the past in the same way, and their subjective view of what happened is just that—subjective. Portelli demonstrated that oral history can tell us at least as much about the past as it can about the interviewee. How people remember the past is at least as important as what they recall.

EXHIBITIONS

Many museums have incorporated oral history interviews into their exhibits in a variety of formats. Some have used quotations from the interviews on panels or as parts of graphic or object cutlines. Others have incorporated the audio or video interviews into the exhibit itself. The examples below demonstrate two different ways that oral history interviews were used in an exhibit. First, we will look at By the Sweat of Their Brow: Forging the Steel Valley, an exhibition at the Ohio Historical Society's Youngstown Historical Center of Industry and Labor. The exhibition is a permanent installation that opened to the public in 1992. As site manager at the time, I conducted interviews with former steelworkers that focused on various life experiences, such as growing up in Youngstown, work life, family, and reactions to the mill closings that began in 1977. Out of more than thirty videotaped interviews, we selected five that were edited and transferred to laser disc. The interviews now play continuously on a monitor in the exhibit hall. The five interviewees represent different aspects of working in the mill. Elma Jones Beatty was a Rosie the Riveter at Republic Steel in Youngstown during World War II. Sam Donnarummo worked at the Youngstown Sheet and Tube Company's Brier Hill Works, where he was severely injured on the job. He was also one of the last workers to leave the plant when it closed in 1979. We also selected Arlette Gatewood, an African American steelworker whose family migrated to Youngstown in the 1940s. Gatewood also worked at the Brier Hill works, was very active in United Steelworkers of America (USW), and eventually worked in the USW subdistrict office in Youngstown. Sam Santinoceto, who worked at U.S. Steel in Youngstown, was an Italian American immigrant. Finally, we included W. Lawrence Weeks, who was in upper management with Republic Steel at the time of its merger in 1984 with LTV Corporation. A short biography introduces each interviewee. A few words introduce each video clip that shows the interviewees discussing various topics such as the last day in the mill, the takeover by LTV, and the like. Visitors to the museum can thus get various perspectives on the steel industry that once thrived in the Mahoning Valley. Juxtaposed with the exhibition itself, the interviews put a human face on the story of the steel industry and deindustrialization.

The Smithsonian Institution's National Museum of American History incorporated oral histories in an exhibition on Japanese internment during World War II entitled A More Perfect Union: Japanese Americans and the U.S. Constitution. The Smithsonian included the video interviews in its exhibit as well. The difference between the Smithsonian exhibit and the Youngstown exhibit was that the former allowed the visitor a degree of hands-on interaction. Topics included the process of internment, life in the camps, work, loyalty, and other related areas. The visitor could decide which interviewee he or she wished to hear and which question he or she wanted to hear the response to. In Youngstown, on the other hand, the visitor can only watch the interviewees. Both museums, however, effectively integrated oral histories into their respective and relatively low-tech exhibitions.

The Community Within oral history exhibit opens in Mount Vernon, Ohio. The project provided local African Americans an opportunity to present their history and experiences—a story that had remained largely untold in local history books and museum exhibits. *Courtesy of the Rural Life Center, Kenyon College*

ELECTRONIC MEDIA

Audio

Radio has long mined oral history interviews for documentaries, which can reach a relatively large audience and are engaging and interesting. Some documentaries such as the half-hour 2002 National Public Radio (NPR) production entitled *Radio Diaries: An Oral History of the WASPs* use mainly oral interviews to present their topic. In 2005, the Ohio Humanities Council funded a radio program on NPR affiliate WYSU-FM at Youngstown State University (YSU) in which students in Dr. Rosemary D'Apolito's Urban Sociology course interviewed ordinary people about their experiences visiting downtown Youngstown during its heyday in the mid-twentieth century. Interviewees related their experiences shopping in the two large downtown department stores (Strouss-Hirshberg and G. M. McKelvey), going to see films at the long-gone movie theaters such as the Palace, eating in the myriad of restaurants, and other activities associated with visiting downtown.

Howard L. Sacks's Rural Life Center at Kenyon College offers another example of radio documentaries as he discusses in chapter 1. Sandra Sleight-Brennan at Ohio University has done many radio documentaries, including *Countdown to the Millennium,* which focused on the working-class history of the coal-mining region of southeastern Ohio. Topics included company towns, ethnicity, union organizing, and other industries in the region.

The aforementioned are excellent examples of locally produced and regionally delivered radio shows. At the national level, NPR, in conjunction with the Library of Congress, has sponsored a program called StoryCorps, in which people from all walks of life throughout the country tell their stories in the project's traveling recording booth. This democratizing of oral history theoretically makes it accessible to anyone who wishes to share his or her life. The interviews will be archived at the American Folklife Center at the Library of Congress. Besides being broadcast over NPR, the interviews can be accessed on the Web or by downloading podcasts.

Video

National Distribution. Oral history is an integral part of many video documentaries. Certainly, Ken Burns's multipart histories on baseball, jazz, and World War II greatly benefited from interviews. Who can forget the inimitable Negro League baseball player Buck O'Neill as he told stories about playing in an era of discrimination, when major league baseball refused to hire African American ballplayers, no matter how talented they were? The eloquent O'Neill brought poignancy and depth to the saga of America's pastime. *Jazz* featured interviews with numerous musicians and other jazz artists. Burns's *The War* made liberal use of oral histories; the Web site also provides information on how to use oral history in the classroom for students to conduct their own interviews.[2]

Oral histories have enriched many other documentaries on topics that range from American presidents to popular culture mainstays like *Gone with the Wind.* PBS, of course, is not the only beneficiary of such documentaries. The History Channel certainly gained viewership with its myriad documentaries, many of which use oral history interviews. Even the all-movie channel, Turner Classic Movies, produces documentaries about the motion picture industry that are enhanced by interviews.

Regional/Local Distribution. Oral history interviews can enrich video productions for local and regional audiences as well. Nonprofit organizations such as educational institutions and museums have also produced video documentaries featuring oral history interviews. One interesting project produced by Indiana University in Bloomington, Indiana, called *The Classics Come Home,* was about the Auburn-Cord-Duesenberg classic car festival held every Labor Day weekend in Auburn, Indiana. The documentary, which was broadcast on Indiana University's PBS affiliate WTIU, used interviews with people who collect, restore, and show classic automobiles as well as people who live and work in the Auburn area who discussed the impact of the festival on their community.

The Kentucky Oral History Commission, which is part of the Kentucky Historical Society, produced a documentary for Kentucky Educational Television (KET) called *Living the Story:*

Children listen in on auction day at United Producers in Mount Vernon, Ohio. With advances in digital audio technology, audio and video stations are becoming common features in oral history projects. *Courtesy of the Rural Life Center, Kenyon College*

The Civil Rights Movement in Kentucky. The producers began with more than 175 interviews of veterans of the civil rights movement in the Bluegrass State, conducted by Betsy Branson and Tracy K'Meyer. The producers selected fifteen of these interviews to incorporate in their documentary. Besides broadcasting the documentary, KET also maintains a Web site that provides information about the production, samples of the interviews, teacher's guide, and tips for conducting oral history interviews.

THEATRICAL PRODUCTIONS

Live theater is another venue for oral history interviews. The beauty of adapting interviews for the stage is that the technical quality is not as crucial as it is for broadcast media or even audio streaming on the Web. Playwrights can work from transcripts as easily as from the original taped source. Indeed, many theatrical productions can be produced on a shoestring as opposed to the far more costly documentaries, especially videos.

The Wallpaper Project is an excellent example of oral history as theater. In 1997, Rachel Barber, the project's director and driving force, began collecting oral histories in Auglaize County in western Ohio. She interviewed people from all walks of life and incorporated their stories into a theatrical production. The first production was *Five Layers of Wallpaper,* which got its title from an interviewee who talked about literally finding money in a wall of a house behind five layers of wallpaper. Since the first production, the Wallpaper Project produced *When the Day Is Through* and *(Ordinary) Heroes.* In 2003, Rachel took the Wallpaper Project to the state of Ohio, where other communities produced oral history plays using their own interviews as well as ones already produced by the Wallpaper Project. The statewide productions were a part of the celebrations around Ohio's 2003 Bicentennial.

Oral history can be presented in many formats. Since 1997, the Wallpaper Project in west central Ohio has been producing plays based on oral history transcripts. Here, community members rehearse with their director in Pomeroy, Ohio, for a touring production of *From Here: A Century of Voices from Ohio by Eric Coble.* *Courtesy of the Wallpaper Project*

The Wallpaper Project's staging was relatively simple. The actors—many of whom were drawn from the community—read selections from the interviews in character. There was only one person onstage or several people interacting. Some of the themes included World War I and World War II, the rise of the Ku Klux Klan in the 1920s, the Great Depression, and other aspects of twentieth-century history and culture. The actors ranged in ages from young teens through the elderly and represented the diversity of American society. The Ohio Humanities Council was one of the principal funders of the Wallpaper Project; other sources of money included the George Gund Foundation and the Martha Holden Jennings Foundation. The Wallpaper Project received a consultation grant from the National Endowment for the Humanities for the statewide project.

ORAL HISTORY AND THE WEB

The Internet has become an increasingly important forum for disseminating oral history in a variety of formats that include lists of projects and interviews available at a variety of institutions, transcripts, and audio clips. The Web offers ways to incorporate oral histories into virtual exhibits and provides research tools for scholars and others who do not have to travel to the actual library or archive. For the hosting organization, Web development can be a more cost-effective way to make its interviews available literally to the whole world. With other new technologies such as podcasts, oral histories can reach whole new audiences who might not necessarily read a transcript, visit a museum, or go to a Web site to view a virtual exhibition.

Making oral history transcripts available online provides a valuable service, especially for researchers. As a case in point, I will use the Oral History Program, which I direct at YSU. Several years ago, Tom Atwood, the former director of YSU's Maag Library, came to me with a proposal to have the library digitize all of our oral history transcripts. I thought it was a great idea; at the time we had transcribed about fourteen hundred interviews that had been collected since 1974. The transcripts were converted into the Adobe PDF format and made accessible through the Maag Library Web site. The user has only to go to the pull-down menu for the oral history collection, and the page displays an alphabetical listing of all the subjects. The user clicks on the subject, and a list of all the interviews on that subject comes up. When the user clicks on an interviewee's name, the catalog information comes up, including a link to the transcript's PDF file. The library is in the process of digitizing the audiotapes themselves and making them accessible through the digital Maag Web site. The beauty of the YSU site is that the user not only has access to the transcript but also will eventually be able to listen to the audio.

Many institutions that collect oral histories maintain a presence on the Web, where the user can read transcripts, listen to audios, view videos, or do some combination of the three. For example, the Lyndon Baines Johnson Library and Museum allows users to read the transcripts online and—even better—actually search all the digitized transcripts (not just one at a time) using key words. The Regional Oral History Office of the

Bancroft Library at the University of California, Berkeley, also has searchable transcripts online. These are only a few examples of the vast amount of oral history resources on the Web, which is making oral history more and more accessible to incredible numbers of people.

EDUCATIONAL MATERIALS FOR K–12 TEACHERS

Oral history can be a very valuable tool in the K–12 classroom for teaching students not only about the past but also about how historians use primary source materials to interpret history. Younger students can listen to interviews; older ones can not only read transcripts but also learn how to conduct interviews. Youth Source, for example, a Web project of the Alberta Online Encyclopedia, contains suggestions for questions children can use in conducting oral history interviews. The site provides information on how to proceed with an oral history project in the classroom and how to critique an interview. The site also offers ideas for other hands-on activities, such as illustrating the favorite part of an interview, writing a poem about it, doing a family history project, creating a play based on oral histories, developing an exhibit, doing a Web site, and producing a radio program.

Many of the projects funded by the History Channel's Save Our History grants program use some aspect of oral history. In 2007–8, for example, oral history was an integral part of projects ranging from documenting the history of glassmaking in Corning, New York, to the African American experience in northern Nevada, to remembering the Vietnam War in Ebensburg, Pennsylvania. In nearly all of the cases, the students not only will collect interviews but also will share their information with a broader audience through such media as the Web.

Oral history is probably most widely used in history or social studies classes, but language arts and other classes will also find it a useful tool. Teachers could make good use of oral history to teach their students a wide range of skills and help them develop critical thinking with an interesting format. Beyond the tangible results, students will not only gain a knowledge of and appreciation for their community's history and its global context, but their work can also give back something to their hometown.

In summary, there are immeasurable things that can be done with oral history interviews. Many times, the end products transcend the original intent of the people who actually collected the interviews. This is especially true of projects that collect, transcribe, and archive their interviews to make them available to anyone interested in them. With the increasing use of digital technology, there are more venues for sharing oral history with a much larger audience than ever before.

NOTES

1. Alessandro Portelli, *The Death of Luigi Trastulli and Other Stories: Form and Meaning in Oral History* (Albany: State University of New York Press, 1991), 1.

2. Public Broadcasting Service, "The Veterans History Project," *The War,* http://www.pbs.org/thewar/vet_hist_project.htm.

BIBLIOGRAPHY

Barnwell, Janet, ed. *Louisiana Voices: Remembering World War II.* Baton Rouge: Louisiana State University Press, 1998.

Casey, Kathleen. *I Answer with My Life: Life Histories of Women Teachers Working for Change.* New York: Routledge, 1993.

Cash, Joseph, and Herbert T. Hoover, eds. *To Be Indian: An Oral History.* Norman: University of Oklahoma Press, 2001.

Cook, Haruko Taya, and Theodore F. Cook. *Japan at War: An Oral History.* New York: New Press, 1992.

Cowan, Neil M., and Ruth Schwartz Cowan. *Our Parents' Lives: The Americanization of Eastern European Jews.* New York: Basic Books, 1989.

Dash Moore, Deborah. *GI Jews: How World War II Changed a Generation.* Cambridge, MA: Belknap Press, 2004.

Dublin, Thomas, and Walter Licht. *The Face of Decline: The Pennsylvania Anthracite Coal Mining Region in the Twentieth Century.* Ithaca, NY: Cornell University Press, 2005.

Gerassi, John. *The Premature Antifascists: North American Volunteers in the Spanish Civil War, 1931–1939.* New York: Praeger, 1986.

Hall, Jacquelyn Dowd. *Like a Family: The Making of a Southern Cotton Mill World.* Chapel Hill: University of North Carolina Press, 1987.

Hampton, Henry, et. al. *Voices of Freedom: An Oral History of the Civil Rights Movement from the 1950s through the 1980s.* New York: Bantam, 1990.

Hareven, Tamara K. *Amoskeag: Life and Death of an American Factory City.* New York: Pantheon Books, 1978.

High, Steven. *Industrial Sunset: The Making of North America's Rustbelt, 1969–1984.* Buffalo, NY: University of Buffalo Press, 2003.

Honey, Michael. *Black Workers Remember: An Oral History of Segregation, Unionism, and the Freedom Struggle.* Berkeley: University of California Press, 1999.

Jones-Eddy, Julie. *Homesteading Women: An Oral History of Colorado, 1890–1950.* New York: Twayne, 1992.

Kessler, Lynn S., and Edmond Bart. *Never In Doubt: Remembering Iwo Jima. D767 .99 .I9 N39 1999.* Annapolis, MD: Naval Institute Press, 1999.

Kessloff, Jeff. *You Must Remember This: An Oral History of Manhattan from the 1890s to World War II.* San Diego, CA: Harcourt, Brace, Jovanovich, 1989.

Knight, Carrie. *The Carousel Keepers: An Oral History of American Carousels.* Granville, OH: McDonald and Woodward, 1998.

Kuhn, Cliff. *Contesting the New South Order: The 1914–1915 Strike at Atlanta's Fulton Mills.* Chapel Hill: University of North Carolina Press, 2001.

LaForte, Robert S., et. al., eds. *With Only the Will to Live: Accounts of Americans in Japanese Prison Camps, 1941–1945.* Wilmington, DE: SR Books, 1994.

Lee, Joann Faung Jean. *Asian-Americans: An Oral History of First to Fourth Generation Americans.* New York: New Press, 2008.

Lewin, Rhonda G. *Witnesses to the Holocaust: An Oral History.* New York: Pilgrim Press, 1981.

Lysaught, Alan, and David Pritchard. *The Beatles: An Oral History.* New York: Hyperion, 1998.

Miller, Marc S. *The Irony of Victory: World War II and Lowell, Massachusetts.* Urbana: University of Illinois Press, 1988.

Montell, William Lynwood. *Don't Go up Kettle Creek: Verbal Legacy of the Upper Cumberland.* Knoxville: University of Tennessee Press, 1983.

———. *The Saga of Coe Ridge.* Knoxville: University of Tennessee Press, 1970.

Passerini, Luisa. *Fascism in Popular Memory: The Cultural Experience of the Turin Working Class.* Cambridge: Cambridge University Press, 1987.

Patai, Daphne, and Sherna Gluck. *Women's Words: The Feminist Practice of Oral History.* New York: Routledge, 1991.

Perdu, Theda. *Nations Remembered: An Oral History of the Five Civilized Tribes, 1865–1907.* Westport, CT: Greenwood, 1980.

Portelli, Alessandro. *The Death of Luigi Trastulli and Other Stories: Form and Meaning in Oral History.* Albany: State University of New York Press, 1991.

———. *The Battle of Valle Giulia: Oral History and the Art of Dialogue.* Madison: University of Wisconsin Press, 1997.

———. *The Order Has Been Carried Out: History, Memory, and Meaning of a Nazi Massacre in Rome.* New York: Palgrave Macmillan, 2003.

Riccio, Anthony V. *The Italian American Experience in New Haven: Images and Oral Histories.* Albany: State University of New York Press, 2006.

Rothchild, Silvia. *A Special Legacy: An Oral History of Soviet Jewish Émigrés in the United States.* New York: Simon and Schuster, 1985.

Santino, Jack. *Miles of Smiles, Years of Struggle: Stories of Black Pullman Porters.* Urbana: University of Illinois Press, 1984.

Santoli, Al. *Everything We Had: An Oral History of the Vietnam War.* New York: Random House, 1981.

Terkel, Studs. *American Dreams, Lost and Found.* New York: Pantheon, 1980.

———. *Hard Times: An Oral History of the Great Depression.* New York: Pantheon, 1970.

———. *Working: What People Do All Day and How They Feel about What They Do.* New York: Pantheon, 1974.

Vickers Lu, and Sara Dionne. *Weeki Wachee, City of Mermaids: A History of One of Florida's Oldest Roadside Attractions.* Gainesville: University Press of Florida, 2007.

Walker, Melissa, and Rebecca Sharpless. *Work, Family, and Faith: Rural Southern Women in the Twentieth Century.* Columbia: University of Missouri Press, 2006.

Contributors

DONNA M. DEBLASIO is an associate professor of history and director of the Center for Applied History at Youngstown State University. For nearly fifteen years, she worked as a museum site manager and historian for the Ohio Historical Society and the Ohio Historic Preservation Office.

CHARLES F. GANZERT has been a professor in the Communication and Performance Studies Department at Northern Michigan University since 1992. He teaches courses in audio production, media management, political communication, and media law, with an emphasis on service learning.

DAVID H. MOULD holds a PhD in American studies and is a professor of media arts and studies at Ohio University. He has experience as a newspaper and television journalist, documentary maker, and international media trainer and consultant.

STEPHEN H. PASCHEN has been university archivist and assisant professor in Libraries and Media Services, Special Collections and Archives, at Kent State University since 2006. He has worked in the field of archives for the past twelve years, and he previously served as curator and director of the Summit County Historical Society for eleven years.

HOWARD L. SACKS is National Endowment for the Humanities Distinguished Teaching Professor of Sociology and director of the Rural Life Center at Kenyon College in Gambier, Ohio. For more than thirty years, he has directed and produced award-wnning projects nationwide.

Index